TALES FROM
· THE ·
FARM

TALES FROM
· THE ·
FARM

AMANDA
OWEN

MACMILLAN

First published 2021 by Macmillan
an imprint of Pan Macmillan
The Smithson, 6 Briset Street, London ECIM 5NR
EU representative: Macmillan Publishers Ireland Ltd,
Mallard Lodge, Lansdowne Village, Dublin 4
Associated companies throughout the world
www.panmacmillan.com

ISBN 978-1-5290-7475-8

7 9 8

A CIP catalogue record for this book is available from the British Library.

Typeset by Ambar Galan
Printed and bound by CPI Group (UK) Ltd, Croydon, CRO 4YY

Visit **www.panmacmillan.com** to read more about all our books
and to buy them. You will also find features, author interviews and
news of any author events, and you can sign up for e-newsletters
so that you're always first to hear about our new releases.

TALES FROM
· THE ·
FARM

Introduction

For two years now I have written a monthly column in *The Dalesman* magazine, and what a joy it has been. I have had some real fun along the way, updating readers with what is happening on the farm – ranging from the sublime (observations of nature and our glorious Yorkshire countryside), to the ridiculous (whitewashed cows, concrete-coated peacocks and children running amok). It really has been a rollercoaster ride, taking people with me on a journey while not knowing myself where it will lead or what will come next (particularly given that each column has to be written in advance, so things on the farm may very well have changed once again by the time it has been published!). And being able to recount these tales is a cathartic experience.

The Dalesman itself needs little in the way of an introduction. This iconic monthly publication is packed with interesting and insightful articles and must be one of the most universally recognized magazines in the country. From the glossy cover right through to the back page it offers fascinating glimpses into the heritage and history of Yorkshire, stories from the countryside, rural life and much more. Over the years it has featured articles written by some of our county's most illustrious names, so it was with a certain degree of trepidation that I accepted an invitation to become one of its regular monthly columnists. I needn't have worried. I feel a sense of connection with *The Dalesman*'s dedicated readership, and it's not just that we share a deep love of our county. I believe that we have an understanding. I can relax and speak colloquially in my own voice (complete with dialect), and it is that familiarity that makes this magazine a special one to me.

My monthly columns have been collected into this new, delightfully illustrated book, and I hope very much that reading it will inspire many more people to look to *The Dalesman* for a breath of that bracing Yorkshire fresh air wherever they are in the world. As the playwright Alan Bennett once said, '*The Dalesman* has proved to be something of a river; it just goes flowing on – and like a river it is, I hope, unstoppable.'

FEBRUARY 2019

'Winter bites with its teeth and lashes with its tail', or so the proverb goes, and I'm inclined to agree. There are varying ideas about when winter officially ends, but there is no doubt that in the highest reaches of the Yorkshire Dales we have disproportionately more winter than summer.

February might be the shortest of months in the calendar, but it is the one that really tests the mettle of the shepherd and flock. This is the most cheerless of landscapes when frozen, lonely and barren. There is no respite from the brutal icy blasts of wind that roll in across the moors leaving a scant sprinkling of snow, and with it an endless monochrome vista. This is a place that can invigorate, inspire and, at times, infuriate.

My fingers might be raw and my senses numbed with cold, but time spent up here watching the flock is not time wasted. Being vigilant now, keeping a close eye on the weather, is of the utmost importance, for if there were to be any talk of a storm then the sheep need bringing down off the hills and into safer ground.

The flock awaits my arrival expectantly, having been alerted to the impending delivery of hay by a series of whistles; a whistle carries further than a voice and brings the more adventurous sheep that have strayed far afield streaming back towards me, nose-to-tail in orderly fashion, in single file on the sheep trods. These well-worn paths through the heather follow the contours of the land and afford safe passage through perilous ground consisting of blanket bog and peat haggs.

Every day, a fresh unsoiled area needs to be found where the flock can be foddered cleanly. The pale green-blue-tinged hay brings a hint of colour to the scene, flecks of yellow within, fragile petals of dried buttercups, a distant reminder of the warmth and colour of summer. The sheep mill around. Ravenous, they jostle for position, snatching mouthfuls of hay, wisps of which are picked up and blown away, rolling across the moor like tumbleweed in a Western film.

On most occasions it's just the sheepdog and myself, though my daughter Nancy (aged two-and-a-half) still likes to travel in the backpack as I do my rounds, master of all she surveys. That's if she can see at all, as her balaclava keeps twisting around as she cranes her neck, determined not to miss anything that is going on. If I turn my head to the side then I can just about catch a glance of a vision in pink, complete with a runny nose and a look of surprise. The wind blows, the air is cold and her cheeks are rosy, but what a sparkle she has in her eye. I imagine that her senses are in overdrive with the smells, taste and sounds of life on a hill farm.

All of my children have travelled via this conveyance; held securely by the straps, they don't move, even when I lean forwards to pick up canches of hay. Nancy wears an all-in-one padded suit with attached bootees and mittens that I tie in place with baler twine. Cold hands and feet are a misery I want to spare her, but I have discovered over time that mittens for baby are also essential in the prevention of bald patches on my head. Tearing my hair out over a missing sheep or a bad forecast is one thing, but Nancy's tiny fingers ripping clumps free is a definite no-no.

The landscape might seem lifeless at this time of year, but romance certainly isn't dead in this neck of the woods. Every February, without fail, my husband Clive will save a few quid bypassing the newsagents and craft his very own super-sized Valentine's Day message, aided and abetted by the sheep. With a little thought and preparation he is able to feed his heaf* of sheep in the shape of a heart while I watch this visually spectacular declaration of his affections from a vantage point across on the opposing hill-end. Maybe I should get him to raise the baa (sorry) and request that he makes more effort this year by spelling out 'I love ewe'.

---

* A heaf is the area of the moor which each sheep recognizes as its own terrain, and the only place they are truly happy.

MARCH 2019

There are still a few weeks to go before lambing time, and the yows (ewes), particularly the ones carrying twins, are now showing their lambs. One of the most useful modern technologies that we have embraced is ultrasound scanning. The addition of a coloured scanning mark to indicate whether our sheep are carrying a single, twins or are geld (having no lamb) has proven to be a great aid in keeping the sheep in tip-top condition, as we know what to expect at lambing time and can feed them accordingly. Each yow has duly been marked, for one lamb or two, with a coloured 'pop' on their fleece.

So now on the moor, as the subdued tones of deepest winter finally give way to a hint of spring, the sheep themselves add a little dash of colour to the landscape. Their wool is adorned with a symphony of colours, all equating to a secret code particular to individual shepherds.

A flock mark states ownership of the sheep and has often remained unchanged for centuries; the Ravenseat flock mark is a black spot on the shoulder. The heaf mark distinguishes which part of the moor they reside upon. The rud mark, on the rump, was applied not by my hand but at tupping time by the male – the mechanics of this transference of colour, I am sure, do not need explanation. The timing of the appearance of this mark gives us an estimated due date for the arrival of a lamb.

Next is the smit mark. This identifies the father: when breeding pedigree sheep this is crucial, as we don't want any mysteries. So while it may appear that the sheep are wearing technicolour dreamcoats, it is more about methodically recording information than about artistic flair.

There is a spring in everyone's step now there is a little warmth in the air. The upturn in the weather has given us blue skies, the sun has been shining, and the lapwings, curlews and oystercatchers have returned to us after their winter in kinder climes. Surely they can't be wrong: springtime must be here.

The window of opportunity for sapling planting is nearly over, and so I had a shopping spree on a tree website at the beginning of the week. I pored over the online catalogue. Pretty, exotic varieties caught my eye: cherry blossoms and monkey puzzles. Then reality hit – the peaty, acidic soil, high rainfall and incessant winds meant that it was all to be mountain ash (or rowan), quickthorn and firs. I did succumb to temptation and ordered something a bit different, though nothing too outlandish: a dozen broadleaved parkland trees. Whether they grow remains to be seen, but nothing ventured, nothing gained.

A few days later and tree guards are in place to prevent the rabbits from nibbling the saplings, while some hasty repairs to the drystone walls will stop the sheep, cows or horses vandalizing our up-and-coming plantations. It was quite hard work: the steeper banks were stony, the flatter areas waterlogged. We snapped the shaft of the spade, and Nancy lost her welly in a boggy bit. Clemmy (aged three-and-a-half) amused herself rock scrambling, and then we all picnicked outside. For a little time there was relative quiet contentment as sandwiches were stuffed in mouths, and hot tea dispensed from our Ghillie Kettle. There was, of course, the usual bleating, mooing and barking in the distance and, above, the lapwings whirled and tweeted, but it was peaceful enough that we could watch a vole scurrying about among the rough grass. He (or, given the frantic pace, more likely *she*!) was scampering this way and that. Busy, but with what, I have no idea.

Over the next few weeks, as lambing time approaches, we, too, will be unbelievably busy but sometimes it is good to just sit back and enjoy the view. 'What is this life if, full of care, We have no time to stand and stare'.

APRIL 2019

The Easter school holidays fall late this year and coincide perfectly with lambing time, which is always late in the highest reaches of Swaledale. So, at our busiest time of year, we will have all hands on deck – what a perfect combination!

Every year is different, weather-wise, and so far conditions have been very kind to us; cold, but sunny and dry, meaning that the doors to the farmhouse have been wide open all day every day as children – and sometimes animals – go backwards and forwards between the farmyard, fields and house.

Every year we construct a sheep hospital in an adjoining barn, and this will undoubtedly become full of patients, convalescing after a difficult birth or nursing an occasional sickly lamb. Hopefully there'll be no malingerers, but, as is always the case, there will be a bed-blocker or two – cases that are hard to deal with, owing to a stubbornly steadfast refusal to show any mothering ability whatsoever. The only cure for this awkwardness is perseverance – holding the yow still and distracting her with a scoopful of ration while the lamb suckles. The thought of finding myself with another pet lamb to rear on the bottle is enough of an incentive to keep me focused and determined to win this battle of minds.

Occasionally, the arrival of a sheepdog on the scene can bring out some deep-rooted maternal instincts that will help matters along, the yow naturally standing her ground and protecting her offspring. It really is all about carrot and stick, but with the emphasis on carrot – or, should I say, bribery.

Fortunately, the majority of the flock will lamb outside in the fields without the need for any intervention – out on the fells is the cleanest, healthiest environment there is. A few have been housed in the barn. These are the ones that have the potential to be troublesome – there are some old-timers amongst them, and a few first-time mothers expecting twins. Having them lazing around indoors is convenient in that you don't need to traverse slopes and navigate rivers just to keep a watch on events, but the downside is the limited space in the building. It increases the likelihood of there being a mix-up at the point of birth, so we need to monitor the occupants twenty-four/seven.

We take it in turns; during the day the younger children will happily be the eyes and ears of the place, watching the ovine dramas unfold in front of their very eyes. They'll report back to either me, Clive, or one of their older siblings – who, after years of practice, are very capable of intervening and sorting out any issues that might arise.

When darkness falls and the last of the outside sheep

have been checked, we sort out (argue over) the rota for checking on the inside lambers. Every few hours through the night either Clive or I pull on our wellies and leggings and trudge to the barn to pen up any yows we find with newborn lambs. This can be done almost on autopilot, without really waking up. Then it's back to bed for a bit more rest, and up at first light to do it all again.

It will take a month to lamb all the sheep, but the best part is the involvement of the children. It might be the holidays, but lambing time is really a continuation of the full school timetable – all the usual lessons taken in the classroom moved to a different location. PE, in the form of chasing and sometimes wrestling a reluctant sheep; mathematics, in the counting of them; biology, of course; and more often than not there's an element of problem-solving. Perhaps most importantly of all they are being educated in life skills: common sense, kindness and empathy. Now if those aren't important lessons then I don't know what is!

MAY 2019

'Ne'er cast a clout 'til May is out' is how the saying goes but I'm afraid that I have had to shed a few layers as, although we are still lambing, it seems that summer has arrived.

I have actually begun to develop a classic farmer's tan, bronzed skin from elbows to hands where my sleeves have been rolled up and a tanline on my legs that stops at the top of my wellies. Below that everything is as pasty (and as hairy) as usual. I've been wearing a skirt – usually there's no chance of losing the overtrousers, as when working with the sheep in the pens their horns are at just the right height to inflict the maximum pain and injury upon bare legs – but luckily I've been on mothering-up duties, standing with Kate the sheepdog in the fields and sorting out which lambs belong to which yows. The presence of a sheepdog naturally makes the yows want to protect their lambs, and with a bit of careful manoeuvring I can split them out from the crowd and send them off on their merry way.

We are still lambing, but are also now marking up the older lambs born a couple of weeks ago at the start of lambing time. The myriad of smits (the colour code of marks we put in the yows' fleeces which tells us who the lamb's father is) are now permanently imprinted in my brain. Yellow in the rib, that's Colin; red in the middle of the back, that's Steven; blue in the tail top, that's Dave. Yes, the tups have long and complicated pedigree titles, but who on an everyday basis is going to talk of the merits of Close Hills Rasputin the Third? Instead, they are referred to by more unassuming names. To any outsider listening in it must sound like the most normal of conversations. 'Aye, Steven's done well, we'll use him again' and 'Ron's mother is a grand 'un.' It's never all good, though, 'Colin's done badly, Tuesday neet for 'im [auction].'

The overriding feeling as the yows and lambs head off through the moor gate is one of satisfaction as, for the time being, they are free to roam the moors unhindered. The next time we will see them will be in a couple of months, at clipping time.

Grass day, which is usually 1 May in the hills, is a time for celebration: cows turned out from their winter quarters, and horses, too. Fed up of being stabled and corralled in the pastures, they kick up their heels and head for the hills.

In and among the sheep work I've been trying to have a 'better-late-than-never' spring clean. I armed myself with a large pot of white paint and set off to paint the dairy and the outside of the porch. There was no big plan: having coal fires means that soot gets everywhere, so I just wanted to brighten the place up. I got busy with the paintbrush in the dairy first, after clearing away some very dodgy foodstuffs that had accumulated over the winter. Foil-packed chestnuts, stewed prunes in tins and a huge jar of stuffed vine leaves. When did I ever think that these would be tasty? 'Waste not, want not' is one of my mantras and so the chickens' hen mash was supplemented with the unwanted food. Hopefully I will be rewarded with tasty eggs.

The problem was that the dazzling brilliance of the white paint on the dairy walls left everywhere else looking decidedly dingy, so I had to carry on. The ceilings, the shelves, the porch outside and in – it was never-ending. I think that the task is the equivalent of the painting of the Forth Road Bridge; I could just keep going forever. By the time the last brush-stroke was applied, mucky hand-prints were already appearing where I had begun.

JUNE 2019

The first week of June always feels like a milestone: all winter's woes are firmly behind us, lambing over, grass growing, cows out on the moor and it's now going to be long, hot days filled with sunshine. That's the dream, anyway.

Summer brings its own challenges. The sheep misbehave and keep breaking back into the hay meadows – you're only ever as strong as your weakest point, and our wiliest sheep can seek out and sneak through a hole in a fence or scramble over a low wall with comparative ease. The grass truly is greener on the other side, although it is not the grass they consume on their forays into forbidden territory which upsets me the most, but the damage they cause en route. In their eagerness to trespass they can knock the topstones off our drystone walls, where they lie hidden until July when they are found by the mower. Haytime will then grind to a halt, literally, while the broken blades are replaced.

The wayward sheep trail through the grass, flattening it in their wake with no respect for the fact that, with no artificial fertilizers used, every blade of grass is precious. I suppose, in the sheep's eyes, they are living for the moment, certainly not considering how welcome the sweet taste of summer will be in the depths of the winter to come.

Our species-rich traditional hay meadows are a sight to behold, predominantly yellow with a profusion of kingcups in the waterlogged valley bottoms. The drier slopes are speckled with shades of purple: common spotted orchids, melancholy thistle and devil's-bit scabious. The patchwork mosaic of irregular fields, many with barns in which hay was once stored, is a magnificent sight to behold, and although many are now no longer in use I am proud to say that we still use two or three for their original purpose.

One of our more substantial barns has been converted into what can only be described as a play barn but, before the National Park planners begin proceedings, I should say that it is all very temporary. A ladder is used to access the hayloft, in which crudely made furniture crafted by the children from recycled wooden pallets is set out. The youngsters have spent many happy hours down there building beds, tables and chairs. The last piece of furniture to find its way into this open-plan accommodation was a circular wooden pipe reel that is now a coffee table.

A campfire was lit outside on the evening of the first proposed sleepover and a fine meal was enjoyed by the happy campers, all nine of them. Night fell; Nancy and Clemmy, the little ones, came back to the farmhouse with Clive and myself; the rest zipped themselves into their sleeping bags in the barn and apparently dozed, listening to the sweet sound of the evening's birdsong. What exactly happened next I'm not entirely sure, but it culminated in a mass exodus. There were many different versions of events; some featured scratching rodents, others the screeches of owls and flapping bats. The play barn now resembles the *Marie Celeste* – everything perfectly in place but no one in residence. There have been mutterings of a return visit but on the proviso that I, too, stay the night. We will see about that!

Tony the pony

Every year, at the beginning of June, we make it our business to pay a visit to Appleby Horse Fair, the annual gathering of Romany gypsy travellers. For a week, the chromed caravans, vardos and bowtops form an encampment on Fair Hill. Stalls and vans are all cluttered together, all vying for attention; their wares, old and new, hung on racks or spread out on the ground. There is an opportunity to buy anything from Royal Worcester crockery, gaudy satin bedspreads and patent leather harnesses to bare-knuckle fighting videos and gold-plated dummies. But of course, as the name suggests, it is really all about horse trading.

The 'flashing lane' is a stretch of road closed to motorized vehicles for the duration of the fair. The equivalent of a car showroom, it is here that the horses and ponies are put through their paces: driven in sulkies, never breaking stride; or ridden bareback by youths, sometimes with a passenger riding pillion. There is no Highway Code here; onlookers line either side of the lane, with no barriers to hold them back. The crowds only part to make room for the trotting horses upon hearing the cry 'watch yer backs', accompanied by the sound of steel horseshoes striking the tarmac.

It was here that Edith, Violet and I stood watching the high-speed antics of the four-legged traffic. Already laden down with an array of spur-of-the-moment (excuse the pun) purchases, we were now slowly making our way back to our Land Rover, which was parked at the bottom of the lane. We were wading through the crowd, occasionally crossing the road, keeping one eye out for the next horse to hurtle past.

Of course, whenever we were at the horse fair the conversation would gravitate towards whether we could accommodate another horse or pony. The usual excuse of not enough room did not apply at Ravenseat and, as a mother of nine, I myself had frequently stated that 'one more wasn't going to make a difference'. Today's excuse was, quite simply, 'we haven't brought the trailer', and until halfway down the flashing lane this indisputable fact had served its purpose in deflecting Edith and Violet's pleas. We had stepped aside and up the grass verge on hearing the quickening beats of hooves and the shrill whinnies of what turned out to be a parade of miniature Shetland ponies, tethered together and being led down the lane by a dapper gentleman. He strutted like a cock chicken, waistcoated and with his camel-coloured trilby hat at a jaunty tilt. His ponies were as impeccably turned out as he was – and leading the sleek, shining, mane-tossing pack was a striking blue-grey and mottled-white pony. Standing at only around ten hands high, what he lacked in stature he made up for in presence with a sweet head and a kind eye. Not only had this pony caught my eye, but also that of Edith and Violet, who were now nudging each other and pointing. The dealer, who was perfectly attuned to any signs of interest and a possible sale, stopped at the roadside right in front of us ready to answer my barrage of questions.

A gelding or a mare? Gelding. How old? Rising eight. Broken? Ride and drive. And, crucially, how much to buy him?

Edith and Violet were by now jumping up and down on the spot. Perhaps in hindsight I'd have to say that my heart overruled my head, but in my mind I had already justified this purchase. Little Joe, our elderly Shetland, was on his last legs – literally – so another pony would be a wonderful companion for him, and be able to take his spot when he galloped off to the eternal green pastures.

There was no time for any consultation with Clive at home – anyway, I knew where I stood on that one. I was completely forbidden from buying a horse, and without the means to get one back to the farm.

It was Edith's observation, 'I think that he'd fit in the back of the Land Rover', that sealed the deal.

He did indeed fit in the back of the Land Rover. With a bit of encouragement from the front and a whole lot of grunts and strength from the back, we got him in. I did wonder if he'd maybe travelled this way before, as he did not seemed unnerved by the experience as we slowly meandered our way back home. Torrential rain now fell outside, and for once I was pleased about the condensation forming on the inside of the Land Rover windows, preventing onlookers from spying our unusual cargo.

As we got nearer to home, the conversation turned to what would happen when we revealed our purchase and admitted to riding roughshod over Clive's strict instruction. We need not have worried. Our pony, christened Tony, made himself at home, was claimed by Clemmy, and has never put a foot wrong. What a character he is – and happily he has also given Little Joe a new lease of life, as they are now never apart.

JULY 2019

July, the height of summer: the sheep are now hot and bothered, laid under peat haggs or in shady ghylls, sweating out the baking-hot days. The children are restless, just willing the summer holidays to begin so they can get on with the important business of camping, swimming, horse-riding and, hopefully, a bit of wool-wrapping and haymaking (vocational training via stealth).

It has not been wall-to-wall sunshine as, unfortunately, the weather has been a little changeable this week. Hot and then showery, it has left us in a quandary as to what to do for the best: clip sheep or cut the grass? This isn't just a question of mowing the lawn – we are talking about a hundred acres or so of winter feed for the sheep, cows and horses – so it's imperative that we do the job well. Usually, on a day-to-day basis, just looking out of the window will govern what we do. We can alter our plans according to the weather at that moment but, unfortunately, when it comes to making hay, not only do we need the sunshine, we need it to keep shining day after day.

We are lucky enough to live in our own little enclave, away from it all and, therefore, we don't particularly get to see what neighbouring farmers are doing. Unfortunately, the children keep us informed about what is going on down the dale via their observations out of the school-bus window. A progress report on what everybody else is doing can lead us to make some rash decisions based purely on the assumption that they know something we don't.

Once upon a time everyone was reliant on the weekly long-range weather forecast broadcast on a Sunday, but with the advent of modern technology we can have wall-to-wall weather reports. I study the local forecast on my iPad; Clive looks at his phone. It doesn't work, there's no reception and nobody ever rings him anyway, or so he says – but what he can do is log onto the internet and look at the Met Office weather app.

'It's gonna rain,' I say.

'Dry week,' he says. Conflicting information certainly, but we come to a mutual agreement that it's all in the lap of the gods and opt to mow a little bit of grass and gather in a few sheep to clip, too.

So what follows are days of clipping the sheep, and loading and shifting hay bales; all back-breaking work. My knees and forearms are scuffed and scratched from heaving bales onto a flat trailer; my extremities are riddled with bites from the voracious midges and horseflies that plague us every morning and evening; and as for my hands, rough doesn't even cover it. They sport splinters from thorns, and blisters from the baler twine cutting in. My intermittent encounters with the sheep, ridding them of their fleecy coats, should be a perfect cure for my gnarled hands – but the lanolin in the wool does nothing but make them sting like the devil. Nevertheless, it is all worth the physical toil, for the end result of our endeavours is a triumph.

Turning the super-white, freshly shorn and marked sheep back to the moor after tea is a satisfying task; they always seem to return to their heafs with a fresh spring in their step. The children, too, are keen to be involved, and we are never short of volunteers to accompany us to the moor gate. They will always jolly up the occasion with their antics en route, turning impromptu cartwheels and hand-stands, while the sheepdogs weave back-and-forth chivvy-ing along any sheep that dare to dally.

On one such evening, as the children and I stood at the gate and took a moment to admire the sun-kissed moor-tops of Swaledale, Edith, almost twelve, declared (in what I hoped was to be a pivotal moment of self-awareness) that she believed that she was 'just like you, Mum'. Pleased, I nodded and smiled at her as she stood holding a crook, my sheepdog at her side. The bubble of pride soon burst.

'Cos I've got snot on t'end o' mi snout,' she added with aplomb.

AUGUST 2019

We have finished getting our crop in this week; the barns are now full to the rafters with small, sweet-smelling hay bales. It was cause for celebration when, after a long day's work, we finally stacked the last few bales into the mew. Scrambling about in the roof space on all fours, just beneath the slates, I had found the heat nearly unbearable. I took a moment for respite while Clive – perched precariously on the bale elevator – barked instructions on how to stack the top row tighter, preferably on edge, in order that they could breathe. Cobwebs in hair and sweating from the sheer exertion, I pointed out, huffily, that at that very moment my own breathing was severely hampered. It was fair to say that, as the day wore on, my mind had wandered, flitting around thinking of phrases, idioms and proverbs relating to hay. 'Make hay

while the sun shines', 'heyday', 'hay fever' and, of course, 'a roll in the hay'. This was absolutely never on the agenda, 'a brawl in the hay' being far more likely as the combination of heat, exhaustion, frayed tempers and midges all added to the marital discord.

So, the doors are now closed, and hopefully we will only need to venture back inside in deepest winter. The steepest banks and wettest corners were also mown and the grass, after wilting, made into big round bales of silage. This cut grass is preserved by fermentation, pickled in its own juices rather than dried by the sunshine.

Although palatable enough to the sheep, it always proves to be more appetizing to the cattle. The bulk of these bales consists of seaves (rushes), tough and stalky. The cows will sort through the bales for them when they are rolled out up the fodder gang in the wintertime. Any uneaten clumps of seaves will be gathered up and used for bedding; the animals will lie dry on the cold winter nights.

The soiled bedding and leftover vegetation rot down on the midden for almost a year before it is spread back onto the fields in the form of rough muck. This keeps Reuben occupied for the days following haytime; at fifteen years old, never ever does he tire of driving a tractor. Not content with transporting hay bales on a flat trailer, he will then spend many happy days muck-spreading. A light dressing applied to all of the now-bare fields will stimulate grass growth and put vital nutrients back into the soil.

To say that Ravenseat has become a tourist hotspot would not be an exaggeration as we've had a burgeoning number of visitors to the farm. Once we were purely the haunt of Coast to Coast walkers, slogging it out on Wainwright's trail, and intrepid ramblers wishing to experience the delights of heather peat moorland; now, particularly during the hot spells, we are awash with day-trippers and sight-seers hoping to catch a glimpse of Ravenseat and, maybe, its inhabitants. I can think of no finer place to sit and enjoy the sights and sounds of the Yorkshire Dales but, unfortunately, the heatwave also brought with it unwanted visitors and, ultimately, a crime wave.

We use (or, should I say, used) quad bikes; although much of our land is still only accessible on foot, they are (or were) our main mode of transport around the farm. In the early hours of one morning, our uninvited guests helped themselves to one of our little off-roaders. Fearfully bold, they circumnavigated the barn, sidestepped the dog kennels, and made off with one machine. Then, to add insult to injury, our singularly upsetting and costly rural crime became plural crime when, the following week, the thieves returned and stole the other bike, this time leaving farm gates open in their wake.

The first indication that we had, once again, been robbed came when we awoke to find the pet lambs hovering around the farmhouse door, and Tony, the children's Shetland pony, in the feed store. It is nothing short of miraculous that he did not succumb to the effects of spending a whole night overindulging on sheep nuts. And so, now that the anger has subsided, we have reached the dull realization that the security of our little enclave has been breached and we have decided to adopt a back-to-basics approach. As the police and crime scene investigators dusted for fingerprints, I dusted off the old saddles and bridles that hung in the loft. The farrier was summoned and the horses shod. We will not be beaten and, for the time being at least, we have merely redefined the term horsepower.

SEPTEMBER 2019

The school holidays are almost over. As usual they have flown by, and although it hasn't been wall-to-wall sunshine for the duration there have been enough decent breaks in the weather to let us get in the crop and finish clipping the sheep.

The general consensus is that our summer has been a 'growy' one. Predominantly warm and intermittently wet, the grass has grown and during this time of plenty the animals have thrived. Peeling the fleeces from the sheep when we clipped was a doddle; no bony hooks to contend with, they were well-fleshed and strong. The humid conditions did bring with them a problem that we don't usually encounter – fly-strike. I am not squeamish – one couldn't be in this line of work – but I admit that I utterly detest maggots. After one moorland gather, as we drove the bleating flock of sheep, I spotted the tell-tale sign that all was not well with one of the tup lambs. Flies were buzzing around its horn, it had a drooping lug and was repeatedly shaking its head.

I announced to the children that being a shepherdess was about more than standing among the heather with your sheepdog at your side and the wind blowing through your hair. There were unpleasant but equally necessary duties to be conducted. This was to be one of them. I am not going to go into too much gruesome detail: all I shall say is that the issue was rectified while the children watched the procedure, wide-eyed and open-mouthed.

It could hardly have been an hour later when the guests who were booked into the shepherd's hut arrived, including a little girl, of similar age to Annas, clutching a large pink appliquéd toy lamb. Clemmy and Nancy looked at the toy enviously; Annas seemed unimpressed and glanced over it with an air of nonchalance.

'My lamb's got a heart on it,' said the little girl, sweetly.

'My lamb's got maggots on it,' said Annas, defiantly.

Clive announced that he'd had to tighten his belt. I took this as meaning that we were to be economizing and watching the pennies, but he was talking literally. Being without our quad bikes has left us leaner; we have walked where previously we'd have driven. The horses have benefited from being brought back into work, and gathering the sheep and checking on the cows in the high pastures has been a far more pleasurable experience. The stock, and indeed the wildlife, take little notice of the person on horseback, so you really get to see what is going on: we spied birds, hares and even a lizard sunbathing beside a rocky outcrop. He'd have definitely scarpered upon hearing an engine! Most of all, our sheepdogs have really had to

step up to the mark. They have come on leaps and bounds owing to our increased reliance on their athletic abilities.

I don't particularly relish the idea of the children going back to school. I try to stay upbeat while searching for crumpled school uniforms and mouldering sandwich boxes that were discarded six weeks previously when it seemed like the holidays would go on forever. A feeling of guilt descends when talk turns to homework and the obligatory 'what I did during the summer holidays' essay. I regret that I didn't take them on a foreign holiday, didn't go to the seaside or, indeed, anywhere – the little ones didn't leave the farm, other than the annual trip to Muker Show. The older children ventured further, but not out of the dale. Reuben spent an afternoon helping out with the clear-up after flash flooding hit Reeth in July, collapsing the bridge at nearby Grinton; this was a lesson in itself in the fragility and the power of Mother Nature. And so the children write about their new chickens, grooming and riding the horses, and watching the shooting stars on the night that they camped out. Thinking about it, I come to the conclusion that they never actually left the classroom: they learn a lot from being at home on the farm – the facts of life and death, nature, wildlife, and the rebuilding of bridges, walls and community spirit.

OCTOBER 2019

There is now an autumnal nip in the air, few leaves remain on the trees and the nights are well and truly drawing in. The harvest of the hills is in full swing; the auction marts are awash with sheep. Farmers from the length and breadth of the country descend upon our two local market towns, Hawes and Kirkby Stephen, looking to buy hardy native-bred sheep from the hill farms.

We have spent weeks preening our sale sheep, aiming to have them looking their best as they go into the ring. Untidy stray hairs around their eyes are carefully plucked out with tweezers; the resulting neat look is a direct contrast to my bushy brows, which don't command this same attention to detail. Their faces are then washed; the children help with the liberal application of soap via a big car-washing sponge. Rinsing is a highly prized task: all the children want to be in charge of the hose-pipe. We have even managed to rig up a warm water system as, unsurprisingly, the sheep prefer this. Then a tint of colour is sprayed onto their fleeces, and that's it. It's always surprising that the sheep finish up looking cleaner, yet the children are somehow dirtier. You'd have thought that the soap and water partnership would have worked in unison.

I have invested in a new sheepdog, a well-bred rough-coated type with huge paws, a wide brow and pricked ears, from behind which grows a mane of coarse hair. He is as big in personality as he is in physical stature. I went to look at him at home; he put on a good show in the hands of the vendor, taking great lolloping strides around the field. A sharp whistle stopped him in his tracks and he held the sheep up nicely without ever biting or snapping at their heels. A week's trial was agreed upon, whereby I got the chance to see how he performed for me. Initially he did everything wrong, but his easy-going nature and his kind temperament when around the children meant that we shook hands on a deal to keep Taff. He's a good dog, although he won't win any awards for initiative. Miles and Sidney were keen to work with the dogs and I knew nothing would go wrong if they went out with Taff.

We have recently speaned (weaned) our gimmer (female) lambs that we are keeping to replenish our flock, and they have also been receiving attention. They can look forward to a winter holiday in kinder climes – but before they embark on their journey to the sunnier, warmer and (essentially) grassier Eden Valley they need their vaccinations. They will stay away for the duration of the winter, returning to Ravenseat in April when, hopefully, the snow will have melted and spring will have arrived.

It isn't just the gimmer lambs that have headed for pastures new, as Raven, my oldest daughter, has also left the relative safety of the fold. University beckons, promising bright lights and a new civilized life in York where she will study bio-medicine. Although distance-wise not too far away (I have been reliably informed that laundry can be brought home on a weekend) and reassuringly still northern enough that dinnertime is at dinnertime and teatime at teatime, it is, nevertheless, worlds apart from our life in Swaledale.

Before she left, we were told that her bed must remain untouched, and her dog allowed to sleep in its usual spot, at the bottom of the duvet.

In fact, the very thought of leaving Pippen, her elderly terrier, had given her pangs of homesickness – unlike the idea of leaving her loving parents and siblings behind. It was while we were sitting on the sofa discussing the details of her departure that Chalky, the other terrier, marched purposefully into the living room, tail aloft, seemingly very pleased with herself as she triumphantly held a mummified dead rat in her mouth. No one batted an eyelid. Raven conceded that, although there's no place like home, there were certain aspects of life at Ravenseat that she would not miss.

The stream of walkers and visitors to the farm has dwindled this week, and from now on we concentrate our efforts solely on the sheep: six months of dealing with tourists will be followed by six months of solitude. It is, of course, over the coming half-year that the sheep need their shepherd the most and, although I don't wish to seem anti-social, I am thoroughly looking forward to it.

NOVEMBER 2019

Hallowe'en is usually a non-event for us. Living in such a sparsely populated place makes trick-or-treating hard work; long walks in the dark across the moors for little recompense.

Having a friend, Herbie, who is a celebrated grower of all things supersize, we are treated annually to a few huge mutant vegetables, enormous enough to be astounding but not big enough to win any prizes. This year we were gifted an onion, a couple of leeks and the seasonal favourite, a pumpkin! The family's excitement at carving the infernal thing into a face soon wanes at the awful realization that when teatime comes they are going to be confronted with a dish comprising its scooped-out innards. Being a big believer in waste-not-want-not, I always try to make something edible out of the pumpkin, but it invariably tastes horrible. I'm going all-out to encourage Herbie to broaden his horizons and cultivate a prize-winning turnip next year; at least they taste good.

There's a lot to do with the sheep at the moment, preparing the yows for tupping time. They naturally have very woolly tails, and to ensure that there are no (ahem) 'access issues' we trim the wool off the top. For us, the breeding season doesn't start until mid-November: spring comes late in the hills, so we don't want any lambs born until the middle of April.

We have bought and sold sheep for the past few weeks, but we have not made a fortune, nor spent one; unsurprisingly, there is a lot of uncertainty in the market at the moment. There are, and always have been, enormous fluctuations in the livestock trade, and at the moment there are fewer people wanting to invest in pedigree breeding stock when leaving the EU means there is the looming prospect of tariffs on the export of meat. We, at the top of our hill, are at the top of the chain – our hands tied, metaphorically speaking, as in the uplands we cannot farm anything other than sheep, and native-bred ones at that.

As I've said, our flock is a heafed one: they graze the moors, held on their own patch not by any physical boundaries but by a natural inbred homing instinct. The flock of sheep is ours in terms of responsibility, but realistically we are merely their custodians; they come with the farm. You take on the flock with the tenancy and, should you ever leave, the sheep remain. There is no option to 'do something else'. So, for the time being, we must just weather the storm – which is something that we are quite adept at, living where we do!

Clive has finally had his long-awaited hip replacement; all has gone well but he is finding the post-operative convalescence tedious. Temporarily at a standstill, with his limited mobility, he is overseeing the process of drawing up the yows to the tups in a merely advisory capacity, and he is not happy about it. For the time being, it is me working the shedding gate and deciding who is going in which field with which tup. He can only bark instructions from his perch on straw bales beside the pen. Sometimes I hear, sometimes not. My woolly hat does seem to muffle or even cancel out his dulcet tones.

Poor Clive, he is champing at the bit, wanting to be out and about and on the move again. I gently reminded him that with no quad bike he was going to be either walking or on horseback.

'Might struggle to get my leg over,' he complained. There's no easy reply to that one!

DECEMBER 2019

December is here. Where has the year gone? It seems to have flown by. It is decidedly chilly outdoors – and, for a time, indoors too, when the kitchen range broke down. Dependable and unwavering, it usually just chugs away, kettles simmering on the hotplate, hats and gloves drying on the back-plate, towels warming on the rail. Throughout the day we come in and out of the kitchen, whether for a cup of tea, to pick up extra layers or just to thaw out our frozen fingers and toes. With impeccable timing, it stopped working the week before the Christmas festivities with no warning whatsoever – to my dismay, and to the delight of sixteen-year-old mechanic-in-the-making Reuben. Reuben disembowelled the wretched thing and found out what was wrong, but couldn't make the fix. At least he was able to tell the repair man what spare part was needed.

We had only just got the range working again when I had water trouble (not of the personal nature, just the type whereby nothing was coming out of the taps). This time it appeared that something (we suspected a frog) had caused a blockage in the pipe, and was the reason that we could be found scrabbling about on our hands and knees unearthing the half-mile-long pipe at random intervals to try to find where Kermit's corpse was. When we found it, it looked like a tea bag with legs.

There was blessed relief when, finally, water was flowing again, albeit a little more peaty-coloured than usual due to there being an airlock, and the tank sediment getting stirred up. Sidney (aged eight) got two notes home from school the next day, the first one saying that he'd sustained a minor injury due to a juggling accident, the second one stating that he should not bring pond water to school in his reusable drinks bottle!

Christmas at Ravenseat is a measured affair, with no last-minute panicking about presents. This is because expectations are low. I promise you that I am no Scrooge, but with a sizeable family who, really speaking, want for nothing, it will be token gifts all round. Small somethings for the children to unwrap on Christmas morning will suffice. I can guarantee that before the big day is over the children will be outside playing on the hay bales or tinkering in the workshop. As for Christmas dinner, I have no fear of cooking a huge meal – every day sees me catering for ten so it's business as usual. There are always a few extra mouths to feed too. Waifs and strays at the Christmas dinner table, isn't that what it's all about? Undoubtedly, I will have succumbed to temptation and have bought the biggest – and, therefore, cheapest – turkey at the poultry sale at our local auction mart.

'What sort of idiot would want a mutant forty-pound

bird?' people will mutter. 'It won't even fit in a normal oven and if it does then it'll take forever to cook and you'll be eating it for months.'

Enough said.

The Christmas tree has been uprooted again and is now up in the living room and decorated, heavily adorned with glass baubles at the top but sparse at the bottom with just felt animals and other more robust decorations that can stand being yanked off by Nancy or chewed by the dogs. There are sparkling Christmas lights strung between the beams; tinsel and garlands adorn the various stuffed animals that stare down from the walls. Candles are set around the nativity scene on top of the piano.

The Bethlehem stable was looking almost as busy as our house with all the usual added extras. Mary and Joseph, kings, shepherds and a whole crowd of hangers-on, including Elsa from *Frozen*. I was very proud of my decorations.

'I think it looks like a grotto,' I said to Clemmy, who then would announce to all visitors that it was grotty, which was probably nearer the truth.

Christmas on the farm is a busy time: there's still all the animals to look after but it is that normality that we like. It is a time of year I feel privileged to be able to call myself a shepherdess. A time for reflection, a time when we count our blessings and thank our lucky stars that we have food, family and friends around us.

Happy Christmas everyone.

JANUARY 2020

We welcomed in the New Year in fine style, outside in the barn calving a cow. It was a perfectly clear star-lit night and freezing hard when Clive and I tottered hand-in-hand across the farmyard. Rather than a romantic gesture, this was in order that we both remained upright. Warmed from within having consumed a generous meas-ure or two of whisky, we were gingerly negotiating the icy flagstones in our wellies.

Clive scolded Chalky, our nocturnal terrier whose bright white, unkempt form had appeared out of the darkness, hissing at her to 'git away yam'. The absolute last thing you need when dealing with a cow, and particularly one that will soon have a newborn calf, is a dog in the vicinity.

We made our way to the barn, Clive's spare arm out-stretched and counterbalanced with a bucket filled with the calving ropes and lube gel. Sweeping a flashlight left and right on the lookout for rodents, I caught the green reflec-tions of sheep's eyes as they nibbled at the hay in the rack that hung from the gate.

In the deeply bedded calving pen at the end of the fodder gang one of our older Shorthorn cows stood pen-sively, staring dead ahead, tail aloft. Both Clive and myself had rather hoped that she would have gone through the birth process unaided but Lady Luck was not on our side that night, and enough time had elapsed since we had last looked at the mother-to-be for us to know that intervention was now required. All thoughts of bringing in the New Year beside the fire, listening to the chimes of Big Ben, evaporated at roughly the same time that we saw a pair of tiny hooves emerging from the rear end of one of our biggest, best cows.

There was no real reason why the little roan heifer should not have been born unaided; indeed it was a mystery why she should be arriving earlier than anticipated. She was certainly afore her time. With a dome-shaped brow and knuckled-over hooves due to contracted tendons, she struggled to breathe when finally her wet, slippery body lay motionless on the straw, steaming in the cold night air.

'Is she a wrong un?' Clive muttered as I poked straw up the calf's nose in an attempt to stimulate breathing. Usually a sneeze and a vigorous head shake, both clearing the airways, follow this most rude of awakenings. Nothing happened in those first few seconds.

'I dunno,' I said, not relishing the thought of what was to be my next course of action.

Clamping the calf's muzzle shut with my hand, I put my mouth firmly over its nostrils and blew – quite hard actually, so much so that I saw her chest rise. Those pivotal moments, probably just seconds, seemed endless – then, from the apparent lifelessness, a blink. Then a gasp, and that was it, life kicked in.

'Whisky fumes,' quipped Clive. 'Enough to bring anything back from the dead!'

All in all, an hour and a half was spent with the cow and calf. We finally came back inside when we had given the newborn its first small feed of colostrum via a bottle.

'Who'd have thought I'd be kissing a cow as the New Year comes in?' I mused as I headed to bed.

'Nowt new to me,' retorted Clive, ever the wit.

We rent a field near Darlington for a few months over winter. On Wednesday I loaded up the trailer and took a handful of our oldest yows there. They enjoy life in these more temperate climes, and are watched over by the field owner, who lets us know if there's anything wrong. Grazing is in demand at this time of year (for the uninitiated, I don't mean snacks to keep your energy up, I mean fields of grass).

I remember one day coming into the farmhouse kitchen and seeing Clive on the phone. I mouthed, 'Who is it?' He gesticulated at me to be quiet.

'Nah, I'm not hearing yer reet,' he shouted to whoever it was on the other end. 'Yer what?'

He is a little hard of hearing, but whoever was on the other end didn't give up and chattered away to a nodding Clive.

'Yes, yes, I'm interested,' he said eventually, 'I'll put mi' wife on, she'll write yer number down.'

He put his hand over the receiver as he handed it to me. 'Someone with some grazing,' he said smiling.

There's a first time for everything, but being cold-called by someone selling grazing was a new one.

I took the phone. 'Hi there,' a voice said, 'I hear that you're wanting some double glazing.'

Ciara the pet calf

Ciara was born during a storm, in a stable bedded deep with straw; she arrived into the world, a brindled roan heifer, steaming in the cold night air. She needed taking care of right from the offset. Her mother, Margaret, is our oldest cow on the farm, the matriarch of the herd, but age comes with its associated problems and we had our suspicions that Margaret would not be able to produce enough milk to sustain her calf. Our fears proved true; it was in fact far worse than we could have imagined, with only a drop of milk in one of her teats.

As Clive succinctly put it, 'She's only firing on ya' cylinder.'

Ciara would have to be bottle-fed. Violet was keen to take over this and the other daily chores involved in her care, basically playing the role of mother cow; little did she know what this would entail. Ciara thrived under her watchful eye and tender care; Violet went out to the stable in all weathers. Nothing deterred her, and of course later in the year, with no school due to the pandemic, they spent a lot of time together – so much so that Ciara became very attached to her human caregiver.

When the weather picked up and Ciara was big enough to be allowed out to graze, we assumed that she would make a beeline for the pasture where the other cattle roamed. We all waited with bated breath to see the moment when Ciara joined the herd, perhaps standing momentarily and looking back towards Violet as though to say a final thank you and goodbye. No such luck. What actually happened was that Ciara ambled over to where the herd were quietly grazing, their heads down cropping the fresh grass. One of the cows looked up towards the pot-bellied calf that now stood stock-still in front of her. The cow let out a moo. Perhaps it was supposed to be a welcoming moo, but whatever it was Ciara didn't interpret it as a friendly introduction. In an instant she turned and set off, tail on end, at full-tilt straight back towards Violet . . . who was also moving at a similar rate of knots, owing to the vision of Ciara – by now a sizeable beast – galloping at breakneck speed in her direction.

That signalled the end of any attempts to reacquaint Ciara with her own brethren: she was Violet's friend, and that was that. Ciara was granted the freedom of the city (well, Ravenseat anyway); she went wherever she wanted, and that could be anywhere. When it rained she would stand forlornly by the farmhouse door hoping that someone might let her inside. When summer came and the door was left ajar she would come inside in search not of Violet, but her next-most favourite thing . . . socks or underwear. Quite why she had an obsession with chewing our smalls we don't know, but at every available opportunity she would head for the living room, where they would be hanging above the fire to dry. Raven soon became adept at performing the Heimlich manoeuvre as she tried to retrieve favourite bra-tops and pants that Ciara was in the process of swallowing.

The arrival of an alpine-style collar and cow bell has finally put paid to her attempts to sneak inside.

FEBRUARY 2020

The weather has been awful, neither one thing nor another. Winter is supposed to be cold, frozen and snowy . . . that is what we like, and that is what the sheep like. Incessant rain and wind is dire, and mud is always bad news.

I was at the top of the allotment on Josie, my faithful steed, looking away across the valley and up into Whitsundale. Josie didn't wish to face the weather and turned tail, her thick winter coat ruffled by the wind; above us a lone lapwing tumbled and swooped. A period of mild weather can easily trick the migratory birds into returning to the hills too soon. So many times in early spring I have come upon the sad sight of lapwing nests abandoned, owing to unseasonably warm weather having tempted the birds back, only to be followed by ice and blizzards.

We ultrasound scan the sheep now to check for pregnancy; year on year, this process is undertaken in the sheep pens with our scanning man Adrian cocooned in multiple layers, eyes fixed on the monitor as he runs the probe over their bellies. Mugs of coffee steam in the frosty air, which is filled with the sound of barking sheepdogs moving bleating sheep forwards, guiding them into the race and finally into the crate. After the number of lambs they are carrying is seen on the screen, a corresponding mark is put upon their fleeces. An orange spot in the middle of the back for one lamb, green for twins and a red spot for none. There's little call for the purple spot which signals triplets. Fortunately it is still a rarity amongst our flock; for a hill yow to rear two lambs is hard enough, and one big hearty lamb born outside in the fields without intervention is what we really wish for.

Raven is flourishing at university; independence is certainly suiting her. Her cleaning and housekeeping skills are still sadly lacking but her cooking skills are impressive. I had rather expected that her diet might take a nosedive when she was entirely self-sufficient, but it would seem that the only change in diet has been less chocolate.

'I really haven't got a sweet tooth any more,' she declared, though I was not convinced. When she was back home at Christmas I saw first-hand what happened after she fell asleep in bed on top of a half-eaten chocolate orange. I have had many varied discussions with her on the phone regarding everything from how much roux you need for a cheese sauce to whether it is possible to prove bread by a radiator. It would seem that her culinary concoctions regularly disappear from the communal fridge, so she must be somewhat accomplished (unless her housemates are entirely desperate). Eggs, though, are troubling her: she states that the shop-bought ones are not up to the mark, insipid and

not at all good for making egg fried rice. If only she were nearer home: we have an egg glut, with Clemmy and Nancy finding them all over the farm, including in Tony the pony's stable and on top of the hay mew.

The children have acquired more bicycles – not of the new variety, I hasten to add, but pre-loved ones that mysteriously appeared overnight on a neighbouring farmer's scrap heap, likely discarded after Christmas. Reuben, our resident mechanic, set to work on them, making a few little improvements here and there: sorting out a seized derailleur that alters the gears, realigning the handlebars and attempting to make the brakes work slightly better. Nothing too drastic was required as the children are adept at handling brakeless farm bicycles, familiar with the slalom technique when going downhill and the dragging of heels on the ground to slow the rapid descents that are commonplace on a hill farm.

It was a surprise when we saw six-year-old Annas pedal past the front door at a controlled speed and in an upright and genteel manner as no one actually knew that she could ride a bike, let alone a brakeless version – she seems to have skipped the 'wobbling on stabilizers' stage altogether.

The bikes would certainly not be fit for a cycling proficiency test but they are good enough to provide the children with hours of cross-country fun, and in this throwaway world it must be a case of recycling in the truest sense.

MARCH 2020

The weather forecasting of late has been exceptionally accurate, and although we cannot change the weather we have been able to prepare for what lies in store for us. We were to expect 'the worst storm in seven years', trumpeted the newspapers and, yes, we heeded the warning but viewed it all with a certain degree of scepticism. We concluded that Storm Ciara could not be worse than the 'Beast from the East' a couple of years ago when we were happed up with drifting snow and battled through weeks of sub-zero temperatures.

Before darkness fell, we had all of the sheep down from the moortops and in the valley. Here at least they could lie under the wind and shelter from the squalls of driving rain. Foddering hay among the rushes would hopefully keep them on the lower ground and prevent them from returning to the higher reaches.

The night in question the winds picked up and the rain came. The sash windows rattled, draughts emanated from beneath doors and the open fire burnt hot in the grate. This we are quite used to, and actually it can feel cosier than usual, cocooned under a blanket listening to the storm raging outside.

The following morning the first sign that it had been an unusually rough night was the pool of sooty water that sat upon the hearth, rainwater having run down the chimney overnight. This put a dampener on things right from the word go, as the water had then trickled onto the rag rug. From the sodden floor covering emanated an odour very much reminiscent of tom-cat piddle.

As it was the weekend, the children would usually have been clamouring for their wellies and heading outside into the farmyard before breakfast, but even before it became light it was apparent that the day was unfit for anybody other than the hardiest souls.

'You have to stay inside,' I told them firmly, 'you cannot go out.'

Even from the kitchen you could hear the roar of the beck, and, across the fields, gentle streams and rivulets that usually flowed harmlessly towards the brook now gushed and frothed, sending spray upwards as the wind lashed across the water. I was very pleased that we had brought the sheep down to safety. I could spy them in the distance, but between them and myself was now an impassable river. It is always difficult to know what is the right thing to do in this situation; they would be hungry and, being heavily pregnant, any disruption to their diet puts undue stress upon them. It was all to consider.

I walked down to the packhorse bridge to assess matters; not much of the arch beneath it could be seen as the water thundered through. The bridge has stood for centuries and would have weathered many storms over the years, but still it looked vulnerable as the waves pounded the stonework relentlessly. The wind howled around me; I stood mesmerized by the speed and ferocity of the surge.

I heard a creak and glanced sideways just in time to see our aluminium trailer, which had been parked beside the bridge, inching towards the swollen river. Water now lapped around the wheels as it moved backwards, edging perilously close to the bank. I stood, rooted to the spot, mouth agape and watched helplessly as the trailer launched itself into the water. The current took hold and within seconds it was hurtling downstream at a rate of knots. This was to be no smooth ride: she seemed quite buoyant, bobbing high in the water as she spun around and rolled from side to side.

Within seconds the trailer had gone out of sight; hours later she was found, shipwrecked on her side some half a mile downstream, back axle hanging off and with not a panel intact, though she was the cleanest she had been in a long while.

Seeing the power and force of Mother Nature at work really brought home how dangerous the conditions were; if any of the sheep – or indeed myself – took a wrong turn and tumbled into the water then we would be swept away to our deaths. Sometimes it is about knowing your limitations and when to accept defeat; the sheep would be there another day.

APRIL 2020

After the relentless storms of the last month the weather does at least seem to have settled down just in time for our busiest period, lambing. I'm not wholly convinced that we have seen the last of winter quite yet, but there are some very hopeful signs that spring is finally here.

On Sunday afternoon I was out and about with the children, heading to the allotment and moor with bags of minerals for the sheep when I saw – and this is where it becomes controversial – a large number of curlews and lapwings. I grabbed my camera and photographed them whirling and diving in the air. 'A curfew of curlews', I tweeted later excitedly. And 'a deceit of lapwings'.

Well that was the start of the furore. Arguments raged as to whether my collective nouns were correct; the grammar and lexical semantics police (what?) came down on me with their full force. Eventually when everything simmered down I acknowledged that whatever you wished to call a flock of numerous birds, shedloads, oodles or suchlike, was always going to be acceptable, and certainly a cause for celebration rather than outrage. A singular, lone solo bird, now that would be a poor state of affairs that we can rage about.

The months of foul weather around Christmas have taken their toll upon the condition of the sheep. Although physically they are strong, despite our best efforts the combination of incessant rain and gale-force winds led to us having a few sheep suffering from blind illness. While foddering hay, seeds from within the bale can blow into the sheep's eyes and cause irritation that suppurates in the wet conditions. If not treated it will lead to blindness. A visually-impaired sheep becomes ultra-nervous when it is solely reliant upon its hearing to alert it to any predators that loom large (Clive and me).

Each day Clive and I would be 'eyeing up' the afflicted, creeping up and wrestling them to the ground in order to administer ointment. Just when it finally looked like we had treated all the woolly patients I, too, was struck down with the very same symptoms. I awoke from my slumbers one morning with itchy eyes. Red-rimmed and squinting, it felt like they had grit in them. 'You've got eyes like our Bryan Ferret,' commented Reuben over breakfast.

Clive delved about in the pockets of his body warmer, eventually fishing out the tube of ovine eye ointment from among the rusty fencing staples, fluffy mints and straw. He offered to dispense some into my eyes; I declined, opting for regular salt baths instead.

The start of lambing time always has its problems, and it would be easy to get disheartened when confronted with the range of ailments that are part and parcel of this particular time of year. Pregnancy toxaemia, staggers and prolapses all add a touch of variety to the usual woes that trouble the shepherd. Unfortunately, one of our older yows was found to be ailing, dull and unsteady on her feet, and we suspected that twin lamb disease might be the cause. This complicated metabolic disorder is fortunately a rarity in our sheep where multiple pregnancies are less commonplace, but nevertheless she was affected.

This illness is notoriously difficult to treat, but after a hasty visit to the vets I returned armed with a miracle cure. Ever hopeful, I dosed her and left her quiet in the stable. Clive was out first the next morning and reported back that the medicine had indeed taken immediate effect and had achieved noticeable results. Then he asked if later on I would put a call in to the knackers as there was a dead sheep needed picking up.

Onwards and upwards, I say. Where you have livestock you have deadstock. Keep calm and carry on.

MAY 2020

Now this is going to be a strange column to write as, since the last article, life as we know it has changed drastically and not in a good way. It would be absolute folly for me not to mention the global coronavirus pandemic that is sweeping across the world, now cutting a swathe through our nation. So, what is happening in this green and pleasant land that we hold dear to our hearts?

It is now alive with birdsong and fresh green shoots of herbage. In the copses, upon the breeze, wafts the smell of fresh hawthorn blossom. On the tops, where frozen parcels of snow remain under shadowy crags and the windswept plateaus of countless moors stretch out for as far as the eye can see, there is an ill-wind, a sense of disquiet in this splendid isolation. In essence, nothing has changed here other than my perception of what is an enduring picture.

Of course, it's early days with the social distancing. It's relatively easy to keep yourself to yourself at Ravenseat, so I am counting my blessings, fortunate to live on what is often billed as one of the highest, remotest farms in England. My vocation as a shepherdess is one of mostly solitude . . . plenty of opportunity to think, wonder and contemplate. Sometimes it's 'I wonder why that sheep over there is limping or tifting', or generally doing something that it should not. At other times it is the bigger picture. Thoughts on the latter could be dark, doom-laden, apocalyptic, were I not so stupendously lucky to live in a 'not-spot': a place with no mobile signal, where I cannot be bombarded with news flashes, headlines and breaking bulletins. But the best blessing of all, therapeutic and refreshing, is to be in the company of the children. Where once I had just two at home, with the rest at school or university, now I have nine! It is fair to say that it is chaos, total bedlam. There are, at this time of year, innumerable tasks to be undertaken on the farm, so there is plenty to keep everyone amused. We are still lambing; there are sheep in the barns, in the fields and at the moor; and the cows are still laid in. Everyone has their own responsibilities, which vary according to age: feeding calves or pet lambs, collecting eggs, mucking out stables. And that is just for starters, because in amongst all this, there's schoolwork to contend with.

In and out of the farmhouse they go, all day; you can tell roughly how many are inside by how many wellies are kicked off on the doorstep. Branches are dragged up from the woodshed to keep the home-fire burning, the terriers coming to and fro as they please, and I've lost count of the number of times I have opened the door only to meet a chicken making a rapid exit. Thirteen-year-old Miles even discovered a hen in the downstairs toilet. He removed her, but only after hearing her celebratory squawk telling us that she had produced an egg.

One Sunday afternoon I had taken a ride out to look around the allotment sheep on my horse, Josie, and as I turned for home I looked down upon the pretty picture that is Ravenseat. The farmhouse, wisps of smoke curling upwards from the chimney. The surrounding steading, packhorse bridges and majestic sycamore tree, all sitting in its little dip. Then, I focused harder, little figures . . . on the porch roof! It is never such a good thing to push a horse hard on the homeward journey – it can soon make a quiet type into a bolter – but needs must.

Clive was pottering about in the farmyard shifting straw in the barrow when he looked up, startled to hear the brisk clatter of horseshoes rather than the usual resolute plod. Reins in one hand, I pointed skywards towards the roof with the other as Josie slowed.

'There on't roof!' I bawled.

'Aye,' he said, dropping the barrow handles. 'Only t'big un's, mind,' he added, by way of placating me. 'Lal un's is fishin'.'

He was not joking either; the little ones were down by the beck with a landing net and a bucket, trying to catch the trout basking in the warmth of the sunshine that permeated the shallow waters. They were certainly not of a size to be of any use meal-wise, but we are not in any grave danger of starvation as I'm well versed at keeping a multitude of people fed and watered.

I like the idea of self-sufficiency. Our own eggs, milk, baking bread, even potatoes have been pulled, so going back to basics doesn't worry me. Rhubarb grows in profusion (near the septic tank), but Granddad always talked of the best, juiciest tomatoes growing at the sewage works and he lived to a 'ripe' old age. Weeds, nettles and docks. Nettle tea and soup are bearable. We have, in the past, harvested nettles and dried them to feed to the horses in the winter as a blood cleanser, good for anything prone to laminitis.

There are plenty of dock leaves to be picked, and dock pudding has been mentioned. I cannot imagine that it could taste anything other than spinach-like, but nothing ventured, nothing gained.

Maybe one of my foraging family will one day become an eminent botanist, and if the nettle soup and dock pudding do not become household favourites, then the harvested leaves of the latter may fill the gap that toilet rolls once filled – using a dock leaf wouldn't nettle me.

So, perhaps one of the upsides of this whole terrible episode that, we, as a nation, are united in and going through together is that we are getting back down to earth, literally. The soil, the land, the countryside, we need it on every level, it can feed our bodies, minds and our souls.

JUNE 2020

A popular, if somewhat predictable, question that I am often asked is, 'What is your favourite time of year?' I guess that I should say lambing time, the pinnacle of the shepherding year when all the toil and labours of the last twelve months come to fruition in the form of bleating, fleecy bundles of joy. But, quite honestly, it is truly knackering. Of course, lambing time is rewarding, days filled with hopefulness and excitement, interspersed with sorrow and heartbreak. But my favourite time comes when, finally, the last sheep has lambed, the final batch of lambs has been marked and turned away to the moor. This happens in June and, for a couple of weeks, work abates.

I mean, it doesn't really, as there's still more than enough to do: the meadows will now have been cleared of sheep, so there's the boundary walls to repair (gaps that appeared during lambing time were temporarily mended with a wooden hurdle and some baler twine). The barns, emptied of all residents, still need mucking out; a midden will be made in a less conspicuous place, as we would usually be besieged with visitors by now.

Somehow, though, the pressure lifts. There's a general feeling of contentment as the ewes are now back on their heafs and have no desire to run towards me in the hope of a bite of hay or a few sugar-beet nuts. Instead, they are wary, eyeing me up from a distance, ready to disappear over the horizon should they so desire.

The Shorthorn cows, the bellowing bovines that for months have reminded me every morning and every evening that they are in need of a meal, are now just brown and white mottled blobs in the black allotment. We count them from a distance as they become feral over the summer. The same could be said of the children too. Small blobs, but pink, moving swiftly in any given direction: no natural obstacles will get in their way as they head over walls and through smout-holes, usually accompanied by one or two terriers. They tend to leave a trail of clues in their wake: discarded sun hats and other items of clothing, tin cups, apple cores or, the other day, a fork (a kitchen fork, not a muck fork).

They too are released from some of their duties. Pet lambs are still being bottle-fed but now live in the garden along with Ciara, the pet calf, who now has just one milk feed a day. Every so often there will be a fine re-enactment of the

Pamplona bull run as the children decide to take their charges with them on a joint outing: they cycle off on brake-less bicycles, pursued by a gaggle of pot-bellied pet lambs, a sheepdog pup and a cavorting calf with its tail on end.

When they return from their jaunts up the farmyard, inevitably with tales of something unpalatable (a dead duck floating in the beck or a dismembered frog in a ditch), there is a parting of the waves as the chickens that usually besiege them in hope of crumbs or corn make way for the breathless entourage. As I watch them, focused and busy doing precisely nothing, I am happy.

We are outside, well aware of the troubles of the world but also sufficiently distanced from it too – I don't mean just physically, but in technological terms as well. Un-touched by the news, out of signal and cut off from all communication, I am privileged to be able to let it into my life only when I choose. If there were to be a few posi-tive aspects to be gleaned from this whole strange scenario, then it is the new connections that have been made in real terms. A community spirit has emerged in the dale, a gen-eral trading between neighbours of eggs, flowers, wild garlic, rhubarb (they don't know about the septic tank) and gin.

Letters have been written to people who I had lost touch with and emails sent to people who, shamefully, I might not previously have had time to communicate with. I was spurred into action by an unexpected email from a gentleman who had family connections with Ravenseat and the upper dale. Would I be interested in seeing a few photographs of the farm in the 1930s? It was very moving to see the impish smiles on those children's faces. Sun hats in place but with that same devilment in their eyes that made me imagine they had just returned from their adventures with terriers and lambs in tow.

How quickly time passes and how fortunate we are to live in such an enduring place.

JULY 2020

July is here, the peak of summer, and there are two monumental tasks ahead of us: clipping the sheep and making hay. It doesn't look like there is going to be a huge crop of wool or hay this year, the sheep having cast their fleeces in late spring and the land enduring an exceptionally sunny, warm and dry May.

The meadow flowers have once again given us a riotous display of colour, more mountain pansies and devil's-bit scabious on the dry banks, but the bog-loving kingcups and globeflowers have suffered from the drought and are not quite as impressively large as in most years.

Our crop of hay is obviously what sees us through the winter, so it is vital that we make good decisions as to when to mow. Quality is as important as quantity, and for this reason we are content to sit and wait for a good forecast; a week of hot, dry weather will go a long way to getting the barns filled.

Clipping the sheep is undertaken over the course of a couple of weeks. They do need to be dry to prevent the wool rotting when packed into the sheets – a wet fleece also blunts the blades far quicker. Most importantly, there is the infinite misery of the clipper (me) to consider – wet sheep means wet legs whilst restraining the aforementioned reluctant woolly customer. All in all, Clive has discovered that wet sheep do not make for a harmonious workplace.

Of course, while bent double, knock-kneed and sweating, there will be a point when you wonder what the future holds for wool. Once a valued commodity, it is now almost worthless, which is a crying shame when you consider its environmental credentials. The qualities of being renewable, biodegradable and forming part of the natural carbon cycle have led to a new and interesting project in which our fleeces are being used to block the drainage ditches (grips) on the moor. Without wishing to prattle on too much about the glories of our county's justly celebrated moors, there is a way that they can be improved upon: by making them wetter. With the blocking of the man-made grips, we can raise the water level, prevent flooding downstream, encourage blanket bog and restore our peatlands. More biodiversity, more insects and birds . . . Some of our most endangered species, the ground-nesting birds such as the lapwings and curlews, are reliant on this habitat as their breeding ground. Eroded, degraded peat moorland is not only ecologically terrible but environmentally too, whereas healthy moorland and blanket bog – acre for acre – locks up more carbon than forests.

With the offsetting of carbon in mind, I really should have been more careful when it came to the new green revolution going on in our conservatory. At the start of lockdown I had waxed lyrical to the children about the merits of growing our own salads and vegetables, without much thought on the digestive consequences and emissions that a wagon-load of French radishes would have on nine children.

It looks like all the offspring will be at home on the farm until September, though there was a brief moment when we thought some of them might be summoned back to the classroom, depending on who had exams. After some initial confusion in trying to ascertain how old everybody actually was it was discovered that nobody qualified and a collective sigh of relief ensued.

I maintain that they are learning all sorts, applying online lessons (yes, they have logged on) to real-life situations. Their classroom now is a mixture of outdoors in the main part, and the occasional use of the computer to gain knowledge.

With no light pollution, we have been able to pick out some of the constellations in our dark skies and can now name the order of the planets, having learnt the mnemonic 'my very educated mother just served us nine pizzas'. Not sure about the educated part but the pizza part could well be right!

I have to say that I am not sure who is educating who really. The children's enthusiasm for wildlife, nature and the outdoors rubs off. All of a sudden, I am happy to commando-crawl through the rushes in the allotment in order to try to get a picture of an elusive curlew sitting on its nest. It is safe to say that we have never been more aware of our immediate surroundings than we are now. Nothing has gone unnoticed; the children have been the eyes and ears of the place. We get daily updates on the moorhen family, the redshank chicks in the meadows, tadpoles in the beck and the shrews and voles that live in the drystone wall.

Maybe the closing down of the normal, hectic world has opened up a whole new realm that, previously, we did not notice.

AUGUST 2020

We have been making hay while the sun shines. My arms are scratched, my fingers sore, and I've been bitten many times over by the various insects that come out at dusk as we embark upon the unenviable task of stacking the small bales inside the barns. Miraculously, the haymaking equipment – most of it what we would politely call of the vintage, or at least of the classic, variety – has functioned without issue. Every year these trusty – no, make that rusty – relics are hauled from the nettle beds in which they were unceremoniously dumped the previous summer and put back to work for a few weeks.

I always eye the baler up with a certain amount of scepticism regarding its ability to work. If it were a person then it would certainly be signed off for the duration, but somehow this year she creaked back to life once again and did a sterling job. It is jolly lucky it did, too, because the farm has lost its resident mechanic, Reuben.

Since the age of thirteen Reuben has honed his natural ability and enthusiasm for all things mechanical and tinkered, mended and codged his way along our line-up of farming bygones. He scaled the heights of our own desperate personal episode of *Scrapheap Challenge*, managing to make one functional hay bob out of three busted ones with only three hours before rain was forecast, and the crop ruined.

But now it is time for Reuben to move on, go to work, earn some money, gain experience among the modern-day heavy plant machinery and get the official tickets that qualify him to be able to . . . tinker, mend and codge with more complicated kit than we could ever need or imagine. He is excited and happy, and I am too. He is passionate about engineering and will go far. Hopefully not too far, mind, as his abilities were not inherited from his father, whose skills tend towards the enthusiastic use of a hammer, gavelock and WD40.

To his credit Clive has a perfectly relaxed stance on our agrikit: he just keeps going, looking straight ahead, oblivious to the lack of tines on the rotor. Occasionally he stops to retrieve a dismembered machine part; though if it is deemed non-essential and of only cosmetic value he will place the severed pieces of metal on the wall-top and carry on regardless.

All of our kit, right down to the elevator that slowly but steadily takes a procession of hay bales from ground level to the dizzy heights of the upper door on the hay barn, was manufactured during an era when machines made a satisfyingly loud clanking noise. We are able to cope when an annual service check requires only a grease cartridge and a tap with a hammer; no downloaded software or hard resets here.

As lockdown rules are relaxed and we see walkers again, there does, at least, seem to be a hint of normality coming back to our lives now – well, as normal as life ever could be here. The place is insanely busy; not actually with any extra people, as we remain closed for afternoon teas, but the general to-ings and fro-ings of the children make for enough commotion in itself.

There are chickens everywhere! We have had a plentiful supply of eggs over the past few months, but coincidentally as the children tired of meals of the scrambled, poached and fried variety the daily offerings of straw-filled burgeoning baskets of eggs seemed to dwindle. Fast-forward a few weeks and we have chicks appearing from behind the straw bales and in the woodshed. Patrolling the loft above the stables is Linda, the angry hen who rules the roost (literally), and woe betide anyone who ventures too close to her brood of nine. Hen-pecked doesn't even come close. Sidney was sent right into the lion's den to retrieve the scythe from the beams.

'Confront your fears, man,' instructed Clive, from a suitably safe distance.

Feathers flew, but a flustered Sidney and the scythe dutifully emerged from within. The hessian-wrapped prize was handed to Clive. What I didn't realize was the lasting damage this was going to cause. Not mentally – there are no bird phobias arisen as yet, and no night sweats recalling the sight of Clive, scythe over his shoulder, shuffling across the yard bearing a strong resemblance to the Grim Reaper. No, the knock-on effect of this episode was only seen the following morning when a screaming Violet (age ten) came into the porch yelling breathlessly that 'summat as 'appened, summat bad'.

She had gone to the stable to feed her pet calf only to discover that its beautiful strawberry-roan coat was now flecked white, and it was sporting a Hereford-style white head. It seems that Sidney, in his hurry to avoid Linda, had knocked over a tin of brilliant white gloss paint which had dripped through the loft floor and down into the stable below. Our calf, mistaking this for manna from heaven, had stood directly beneath trying to catch the steady stream of milk! She was none the worse for the experience and seemed to rather enjoy the cleaning and grooming session that followed but it truly was, I have to say, a complete whitewash.

SEPTEMBER 2020

We always reckon that in order to keep on track and not get behind with our work, we should be 'clipped up' by mid-August, meaning that every yow should now be shorn and have been through the pens.

After sorting up, the yows return to their heafs at the moor with their gimmer (female) lambs in tow. Tup lambs are speaned (weaned) and are now in the meadows; compensation for the loss of their milk supply is found in grazing the fog, the post-haytime bright-green regrowth of grass. This has shot up with the application of a light dressing of farmyard manure, washed into the soil by the frequent rain showers that have thwarted our barbecue plans but gifted us with a bountiful selection of free food.

Blackberries, bilberries (delicious, but too tiny and fiddly to ever pick enough to make a pie) and mushrooms; the damp humid conditions have suited them and we have found some seriously large ones. Not having much in the way of trees we never fare as well with orchard fruits, but I have discovered that in nearby Kirkby Stephen there does seem to be a demand for willing and enthusiastic people to gather up windfalls, and I have plenty of volunteers. Plums, pears and of course

cooking apples are all ripe and ready for the taking, and by just freezing the surplus we have a ready supply for over the winter.

It is going to be a strange autumn. Usually we would be looking forward to the forthcoming breeding sales, but with so much uncertainty in the marketplace we have little idea what is in store for us. The lack of summer shows, too, has added to the general confusion and played its part in muddying the waters. To take an animal that you consider to be a good example of your stock to a show will generate feedback, good or bad. It is difficult to know where you are in the line-up when you have no opportunity for comparisons.

The conviviality of the shows and sales is what we really miss. Every year the show must go on, come hell or high water (which last year, in the aftermath of the horrendous floods, was what Reeth Show had to contend with). Muker Show is our annual holiday, mixing business with pleasure and, for the children, signifies the end of the summer holidays and the return to school. The children will go back with, I think, a renewed enthusiasm for their studies. Whether we will be able to locate school shoes, PE kits and sandwich boxes is another thing, and if we do track down the Tupperware then I hope to hell that there isn't a mouldering yoghurt pot within.

Reuben's school days are over and he is mightily pleased about this. He has entered the world of work after securing himself a job as an apprentice mechanic at a plant machinery dealership. He is in his element, enthusiastic about work and enjoying the daily commute. This might change, of course, when the weather turns. I am not sure how he will cope with gale-force headwinds and drifting snow on a 49cc moped, but we will tackle this when the time comes.

Raven will go back to university. Some of her lessons are online but others involve practical assessments in a laboratory. As she succinctly put it when I asked her how much of her studies could be undertaken virtually, 'would you trust me to wield a needle, scalpel or likewise, safe in the knowledge that I had learnt online?'

So, all in all, we will now have only one child at home, as the formidable force that is Clementine will start school. Leaving her pony, Tony, will be a wrench, but hopefully she will soon get into the routine and be able to entrust his daily welfare and upkeep to little Nancy . . . or at least show her where the secret stash of Polo mints is kept.

Regardless of how mismatched the hand-me-down school uniforms are, they will all have perfect haircuts, as we were fortunate to be offered the opportunity to have our hair cut by a top London stylist. The idea was that the hair (there would be plenty) would be made into wigs for the Little Princess Trust, a brilliant charity that helps children who, through serious illness and treatment, have lost their hair. The salon was to be in the barn where the usual clients awaiting a short back and sides are our fleecy friends, so this was a real turnaround. This time *we* were being clipped. My last visit to a salon was over thirty years ago, so to say I was nervous was an understatement.

However, it all went smoothly; the children and I liked the results, and a decent amount of hair was collected – though, truthfully, it wasn't how I was going to look after the cut that had been worrying me the most, my great bugbear being that only a few days previously I had noticed that a few of the children were itching. I told myself not to worry; they'd been playing in the wool sheets and among the hay, and there was no way we could have any kind of head louse infestation when we had no real contact with anyone else. Then I thought about Howard, the hedgehog that the children had been feeding worms to: he had fleas. I thought about Sprout, the terrier – she had been discovered sleeping on my pillow one day, and she also occasionally harboured fleas. I started to scratch too.

Needless to say, we had nits. I combed the children's hair religiously, spurred on by the fear that the visiting hairdresser to the stars would take back some of Yorkshire's hardiest head lice to his Mayfair salon. Now that would make the headlines, I thought.

'If you mention this to anyone then there's gonna be trouble,' I hissed to Clive as the hairdresser and his entourage set up their equipment in the barn.

'Nope, I won't,' he muttered. 'That'd be a lousy trick.'

I wasn't amused, and he went away with a flea in his ear. Let's just hope that he was the only one.

Clemmy starts school

All of the children have only started school when they absolutely had to, the term after they are five years old, when the law states that formal education must begin. Of course, the children all differ in their characters and ways, and even at this tender age it is abundantly clear who is going to enjoy the experience, and who is going to rail against it. At least at five years old it is possible to explain why school is a must. Clemmy has always been of such a forthright disposition, with her own ideas and opinions, that we had considered sending her to school as a four-year-old as she seemed so confident and ready to learn. Clem had different ideas, stating that she wished to spend another year with her pony, Tony.

'But I'm gonna be learnin',' she stated when we discussed school and its benefits. 'Learnin' how to ride better.'

That was reason enough. Of course, the time came when the school bus came for Clemmy, and she went happily, saying goodbye to Tony over breakfast. There were no tears, tantrums or problems. School became just another routine, though not something to be endured – she truly revelled in the new challenge. Tony, too, became accustomed to the timings of the school day, and would stand patiently at the packhorse bridge waiting for her to return home on the school minibus.

OCTOBER 2020

I had high hopes that there might have been a little bit more decent weather coming our way before we fell headlong into winter, but alas it was not to be. Autumn here in the hills seems to exist in name only; climatically we seem to go from summer to winter with little in between.

Now the rain has come and, although there is still plenty of grass for the animals to graze, we've had our first overnight frosts. It won't be long before the Shorthorn cows are laid in for the winter. As a native breed they are able to withstand a cold night or two, but they soon start to lose condition if the wind and rain become relentless.

Before any of the animals can take up their winter residence, the farmyard buildings require an overhaul. Gutters have been emptied of detritus accumulated over the year, including soggy leaves, moss and tennis balls. Slates dislodged during the storms earlier in the year have been slid back into position, and the cobbled stalls in the stables scraped clear of muck and covered with rubber mats.

At some point since spring rodents had taken up residence in the barn where a few small bales of year-over hay were stacked. This, which we optimistically call 'storm hay', is what we keep for the leanest of days, when things are desperate and anything half-edible will satisfy the hunger pangs of either sheep or cows. Anyway, this particular fodder has been downgraded yet again, as the aforementioned rodents had taken it upon themselves to eat the twine that held the bales together and leave us with a barn full of loose, stale-smelling hay. We have barrowed it all away ready to use as bedding.

Looking up into the rafters of the barns, the children spied a pair of barn owls. Wise birds; they didn't hang around long as the shrieks of excitement sent them flapping off through the loft door.

The terriers had an enjoyable few hours nosing around on the hunt for any vermin that were daft enough to not have vacated the building. The terriers have remained pretty much on the premises this summer. With fewer walkers on the footpaths there has been less temptation to

wander off for adventures in far-flung exotic locations such as Keld, Askrigg and once, remarkably, Teesside. They did briefly, however, have to share their fireside rug with another member of our canine family: Bill, our veteran sheepdog.

Every evening when all the work is done for the day our very last job is to let the sheepdogs out of their kennels and let them gallop up to the river. Five sheepdogs, Kate, Bill, Midge, Taff and Nell all take it in turns to run, roll, tussle and play under our watchful eyes. They are easily distracted and will set off after sheep with no encouragement whatsoever. Heaven help any stray members of the flock that make the mistake of being in the vicinity when this unruly lot are loose.

Anyway, on Sunday night I was just putting tea on the table when a pale-faced Clive came to the farmhouse door. I could see from his expression that there was something wrong. He gesticulated to me to come outside, whereupon all he could bring himself to whisper was 'mi owd dog.'

'What's happened?' I said, fearing the worst.

'He's done,' he said, 'he's done, is t'owd lad.'

My mind was racing, thinking of what we might have to do. I told Miles to oversee teatime. Clive and I went to the kennels, where an unsteady Bill struggled to keep his balance and seemed dazed. We brought him fresh water; he drank. He tried to cock his leg but fell over. I brought him a tin of dog food and biscuits – he cared for neither.

We carried him inside and propped him up by the hearth. He didn't seem entirely relaxed with the notion of being inside the house – in fact his misty eyes seemed to take on a new look of anxiety.

'E'el be dead in't morning,' said Clive as he sat on the fender stroking Bill's head. 'And he don't like it in here.'

'I think that he's had a stroke,' I said as I googled the symptoms.

After careful consideration we decided that the best course of action was to take him back to his kennel, where we made him a bed from a sheep's fleece and left him quiet. The smaller children said prayers for him; Reuben offered to dig a hole.

At bedtime we peeped in at him, only to find him dozing. Counting sheep in his sleep, I would think.

We were up at daybreak, expecting the worst. Bill had other ideas. Whatever had struck him down so severely had left him! His appetite for food had returned, as had his lifelong passion, the pursuit of chickens. We don't really know what happened but we are grateful that Bill, our faithful old campaigner, is still with us.

Seeing Clive walking across the yard, Bill mooching alongside, made me thankful that there's life in the old dog yet.

Bill

A shepherd is nothing without a dog; no drone or quad bike can ever replace the sheepdog. I shall refrain from calling them a work tool, for they are more than that. They are companion, colleague and confidant, but sadly their lives are short. They learn, become accomplished at their art, you know them as well as you'd know a close friend . . . and then, in the blink of an eye, you see old age and infirmity creeping their way into your once sleek, lithe and athletic workmate.

Bill had always been a dependable and honest soul, a real stalwart who was clever, exceptionally tough, and whose dedication to us was unerring. It would be untrue to say that he never let us down, as in his advancing years he took it upon himself to be more of a free spirit. He would abandon us in our hour of need, going home when he didn't feel like chasing sheep any more. I couldn't blame him really – I often felt the same. Clive soon got wise to his dereliction of duties, and would make sure that he took one of the younger dogs along on errands too. I suppose this might have irked Bill a little – he did not like us to share our affections with any of the other dogs, and still right to the very end of his life he was the TOP DOG.

He need not have worried about the other dogs; the level of understanding and intelligence that Bill possessed takes years to develop. I am sure that Midge and Taff will get to this place eventually, but for the moment they are too 'hot', too keen on work to really fill the empty space that Bill has left. Kate really is the nearest we have to a replacement; she is certainly willing and trustworthy, but as yet does not have Bill's power and dogged determination.

A few days after the first incident that I've described, Bill had a minor stroke late one afternoon. He seemed disorientated, his gait unsteady; by early evening, after a discussion with our vet, we decided to bring him inside to lie warm and comfortable next to the fire. The children said a little prayer over supper, and Clive and I sat reminiscing about Bill's finest moments and otherwise.

'D'ya remember how we went down into t'Boggle Hole an' got that crag-fast sheep out?'

'Aye, d'ya remember how he rolled in fox muck an' what he did to that walker's leg?'

Nobody slept so well that night, expecting the worst. Having googled his symptoms and the outcomes it seemed that his life was hanging in the balance. But Bill was the comeback king. The next morning he was standing at the door looking longingly through the glass pane to the grass where the hens quietly scratched. For another two weeks he lived his best life, helping out here and there in the sheep pens when the mood took him, chasing hens and watching the world go by. Then a tiredness took over; he lost his appetite, and one afternoon looked longingly back through the glass pane of the farmhouse door to where we were sitting. He lay by the fire that night and, as the flickering flames and glowing embers in the grate died, so too did Bill.

He is buried by the back door. His presence is felt, and he will be forever remembered, as into a stone in the wall have been chiselled our parting words: 'Bill, that'll do'.

NOVEMBER 2020

November really is an exceptionally busy month. The autumnal saying 'all is safely gathered in, hay is got and cows laid in' makes it appear that everything is done and we can just batten down the hatches and go into hibernation over the winter. In fact the opposite is true: there is more work than ever. Along with the daily routine of feeding and mucking out the cattle, there are now the sheep to contend with as they are down off the moors and in with the tups.

A supreme effort is needed now. Each small flock in every field will be visited daily, all the yows gathered up to the tup to make sure that no one in season and ready to mate is missed. A bite of feed in a scoop for the busy lad will keep his spirits up and give me the opportunity to daub the oily ruddle paint on his brisket. The gentle touch is no good now – a liberal application is required, as he must leave a mark on the ladies' rumps that will still be visible five months later. I need to know exactly when I can expect the arrival of the little fleecy bundles of joy.

Tupping time is an excellent occasion to fine-tune the young sheepdogs: plenty of opportunity to practise gathering the pastures and 'holding up' the sheep. It is now that

I bemoan any gates that do not swing and compile a shopping list of new snecks, hangings and posts. One sunny afternoon, after deciding that I'd had enough of one of the aforementioned gates, I persuaded Clive to mix up some cement and have a go at strengthening the foundations of the gatepost into the cow pasture. He did a lovely job. Everything was carefully repositioned and propped: he even used the leftover cement to fill in the puddled space between the sheep pens and the kennels.

The minute our backs were turned, Tony and Little Joe, the Shetland ponies, had found their way to the field gate. Joe has latterly been troubled with dandruff, though it wasn't to be any head-and-shoulder itching that did the damage. He backed up to our newly straightened post and had a seriously forceful backside scratching session, leaving it freshly askew.

It did make me laugh. 'Looks like the leaning tower of Pisa now,' I chortled.

Clive talked not so fondly of the ponies and of Pisa too . . . his comment ending in 'off'!

If that wasn't bad enough, by the time we returned from that incident the peahen had strutted right through the freshly laid cement by the workshop. Not content with doing it once, she had clearly got . . . well, not cold feet exactly, but perhaps more of a sinking feeling halfway across on the return trip, and had sat down in the middle. Panicking upon seeing a fuming Clive approaching, she honked, did a few animated goose-steps and executed a hasty escape.

Clive was raging by this point. My quips about concrete evidence and fowl play didn't help. He stated firmly that we were going back to the tried-and-tested baler twine. There were to be no more farm gate improvements in the near future and that was set in stone!

DECEMBER 2020

Well, as we now say goodbye to 2020, I can state with absolute certainty that it has been a year to remember, but unfortunately for all the wrong reasons. Usually the unmentionable C-word in this house is Christmas, but this year it has obviously been Covid.

Dear *Dalesman* readers, I have deliberately not even muttered about this for fear that you too will be tired of hearing suchlike, so I am going to tell you all about a few of the positive occurrences that have come about over this past year. Firstly, and I have touched upon this before, the joy of conversation and communication by whatever means available: sometimes a phone call or a text, and, of late, the humble letter inside a seasonal greetings card.

One such correspondence really did prove curious, as it was from a genealogist who had unearthed some fascinating and poignant information regarding my family tree. Being polite, he wondered if I, too, was interested. It was when he enquired as to whether I wanted to know 'everything' and reassured me that it was 'entirely normal to have a black sheep in every family' that I really became enthusiastic about knowing about my forebears.

Apparently, go back a few hundred years and I have a

relative who was executed on the Halifax Gibbet. Rather than being hanged, though, he was beheaded – with a guillotine that was renowned for being incredibly blunt. As the decades passed there was little improvement in the fortunes of my family and I read about ancestors killed in mining accidents, transported to other countries or locked up for nicking stuff. I was excited to find out that there was even a picture of one of my direct ancestors . . . then disappointed to discover it was a mugshot taken before he was incarcerated.

So, were there any notable figures in the lineage? Yes: imagine my joy at discovering that I have a distant relative who was a suffragette and whose picture was on the front page of every national newspaper when, in an act of derring-do, she tried to break into the Houses of Parliament.

The next positive outcome from this most strange of years has been a rekindling of my relationship with the humble house cow. It is a long time since we had the need or the inclination to fill a pail with warm milk for our own consumption, but with less frequent trips to suburbia and a herd of super-docile Shorthorns, it made complete sense to milk the situation for all it was worth.

It's a simple, old-fashioned concept. The cow, Margaret, keeps her calf, Milky Way; we share with Milky Way what she produces, which is an ample amount to keep our sizeable family going. Dorothy is due to calve next, and the children are willing her to deliver as they are very keen to

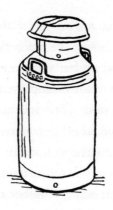

expand our house cow empire. We have a butter churn and a cheese press, so who knows what might be in the exhibits in the home produce tent at Muker Show next year! Until then, though, I must tolerate a constant commentary on what Dorothy is doing.

'Making uncomfortable sounds', was the last vague update on her general wellbeing. That could be the cow or Clive, I thought.

So what else can I say? The house is now decorated for the festive season, but is still in a general state of disarray. Terriers doze by the fire, and cushions are strewn across the floor along with hats, books, socks; it's never going to be tidy, but it exudes warmth and homeliness.

Raven is back from university for Christmas, having announced that, being nocturnal now, she'd be arriving very late at night. I told her that we could not wait up. After all, we now had to be up at the crack of dawn to milk. What I forgot to tell her was that, since her last visit, I had changed the hiding place for the house door key. Apparently, she stood on her tiptoes and reached up into the small recess above the window (I trust that there are no would-be burglars among *Dalesman* readers) and grabbed the pom-pom key fob. After a few moments of fumbling in the darkness, trying to find the attached key to let herself in, she realized that she was trying to open the door with a bat! She promptly threw it, whereby it flew off, she said, and quickly – like a bat out of hell, I suppose.

'There is no place like home,' she mused over a shared late-night cup of tea after I'd been rudely awakened from my slumbers by the commotion and gone downstairs to let her in.

'Are you all right? Happy to be home?'

I was fully expecting a tirade owing to her recent, most unusual upset.

'Yes, really happy. Upset, nah . . . didn't bat an eyelid,' she said. 'I love this place, I wouldn't change it for the world!'

Christmas gifts

It is always a problem trying to buy the right gift for each of the children at Christmas time; ideally we want everyone to have a present that they truly appreciate. It sounds like a cliché to say that it's the thought that counts, but in our case that's true – it really cannot come down to spending an equivalent amount on each family member. Sometimes the right gift might only cost a few pounds; at other times finding something useful might be more expensive.

The cow bell that Ciara the calf wears to warn us of her approach was the perfect Christmas present for Violet the cowkeeper, whereas Reuben, commuting to work on a moped, needed to be fitted up with a mobile phone. It was a fifty-minute journey, and a slow one at that. He told us that one day as he powered up Tailbrig, a notoriously steep hill up out of Cumbria, he looked sideways to see a sheep overtaking him. It would be useful for him to be able to call for help should he break down en route – or at least summon one of us to come and pick him up if he'd managed to procure some random piece of defunct machinery from the skip at work that couldn't be brought home balanced precariously on the back of the moped.

Having asked Clemmy what she wanted to be when she grew up, it had come to our attention that she thought as she grew up, so would Tony.

'I want to be a horse rider and go fast in races,' she said. Raven and I nodded approvingly.

'On Tony,' she added.

In her mind, as she grew taller so too would Tony, and the perfect partnership would continue. I couldn't bear to break the news to her that one day she would be too big to ride him, and that Tony was destined to forever have the bodily dimensions of a small fridge.

There was a solution to this problem, a way of keeping Clemmy's dream alive and keeping Tony busy too – a horse-drawn trap. It would be the perfect Christmas present, and one that all of the children would get enjoyment from.

'Is Tony broken to harness?' Raven asked.

'Absolutely he is,' I said. '"Ride and drive" said the dealer.'

'Hmm, he'd have also told you that Tony could touch-type if it got him a sale,' she replied.

We soon sourced a second-hand mini Shetland carriage. After a few small alterations, and the adaptation of an antiquated harness from our own barn loft, we were champing at the bit and ready for the off. Or at least Tony was.

Christmas morning arrived and the carriage was set ready for Clemmy, Annas and Nancy to find when they made their morning trip to the stables. Myself, Clive and the older children (who were in on the Christmas present) all hovered around the door waiting for the moment when the surprise was discovered. We heard the whoop of joy.

'What have you got, Clem?' I asked. She could hardly speak through excitement, while Nancy was jumping up and down on the spot.

'It's . . . it's a . . . it's a wheelchair for Tony!' Clemmy squealed. 'For when he's really tired after a race. I'll be able to push him!'

I couldn't breathe with laughing, and it has to be said that, regardless of who is in the driving seat, it will make them both very happy for many years to come.

JANUARY 2021

The somewhat muted Christmas festivities are well and truly behind us, and we are now into the New Year and what feels like is going to be an exceptionally bleak January. The cold is jarring; the wind seems to be coming out of the north, bringing with it a continual threat of snow.

We are settled into our winter routines: we start with the chores around the yard, bedding up and feeding the cattle, horses and the tup hoggs (male lambs that have weaned). We milk the house cow, thaw pipes and shovel the proverbial. Then, after more mugs of tea and some layering up, we go our different ways, Nancy usually opts for accompanying me, but with Raven still studying from home there are times when she stays inside and joins her for an online lecture.

The sheep wait for us under the steely grey skies, contentedly grazing the benty ground where we fodder them daily with bales of sweet-smelling meadow hay. Our familiarity with the land means that both Clive and I know the perils and pitfalls of the moor, our territory. We watch the weather and move the sheep accordingly: out of the wind, under the scars or away from the gullies and ghylls if need be.

So it is with a degree of excitement and trepidation that we have taken on some new pastures and traditional barns

– and with this land come moorland rights to graze 150 sheep and five cows. Establishing a new heaf of sheep at the moor and exercising these rights on the common is quite an undertaking, and not nearly as simple as it may sound; the sheep need to develop the homing instinct that will tie and hold them on our boundary-less patch of earth.

We have selected some of our younger sheep to be the foundation of this venture, marked them up accordingly to distinguish them as a new flock, and moved them to their new heaf. At the moment we are visiting them twice daily with hay and sugar beet, trying to hold them through bribery, and so far so good.

Quite what will happen should a snowstorm hit I am not so sure, as I suppose that they are, in a way, as lost and disorientated as I am in this new ground. It could takes years for the sheep to really develop that sense of belonging but it will come, as sure as eggs is eggs . . . which brings me nicely onto the subject of chickens.

A new addition to the seemingly never-ending line-up of things wanting food are the hens, who are now incarcerated owing to the bird flu outbreak. Usually their diet consists of a bucket of hot mash in the morning, topped up with scavenged leftovers while out and about around the farmyard, but now we have to feed them morning and night. I'm sure the lack of daylight is the reason their yolks are so insipid.

Miles is our resident chicken fanatic and thus every afternoon, no matter the weather, he will head out to the optimistically named poultry unit, where the hens are currently confined, in the hope of finding an egg or two.

Fortunately, he is used to disappointment, it just isn't rich pickings at the moment. Clemmy, however, had better luck in the stables, where Linda, our feisty chicken with attitude, has taken up residence in the hay manger.

Clemmy's unshakable determination to collect the prize, an egg that was well out of her reach, resulted in a true masterpiece of ingenuity. It began with the bribery of Tony, our Shetland pony with a 'healthy' appetite. (I would say that he eats like a horse, but he would, wouldn't he?)

Anyway, Tony is of ample proportions, with a back like a table top, which can also serve as a stepping stone upon which to balance in pursuit of an egg. Strategic placement of carrots tempted Tony to stand under the manger; a quick scramble (sorry) had a barefoot Clemmy stood, precariously balanced, on his back. With some nimble manoeuvres she could get her small hand through the bars, into the nest and under Linda's feathered undercarriage, and claim the egg long before Tony was anywhere near finishing his meal.

This became a nightly occurrence and things went relatively smoothly for a week, poetry in motion, man and beast (and chicken) working together in perfect harmony. Until Friday when, inexplicably, Tony lost his appetite,

Linda lost the plot and Clemmy lost her balance and was left with egg on her face – literally.

I should add that no animals were harmed during this escapade and Clemmy, too, saw the funny side once she'd recovered from the shell shock!

FEBRUARY 2021

Winter has finally caught up with us; we are waking up each morning to fresh snowfall. There has been no fearful forecasting of a terrible storm, just day after day of what began as gentle, harmless snow; cold, bright days and overnight sub-zero temperatures. It had been wonderful, like a proper winter. The powder-dry snow dusted the children's hats and coats as they sledged and snowboarded down the pastures, never dampening their enthusiasm or their backsides as they inevitably ended up sprawled out long before they reached the bottom of the field.

Every morning a fresh, pure layer of snowfall awaited them and a number of igloos were built in the garth. The arrival of laptop computers from school led to the general expectation by the schoolteachers that the children were going to be logging in, online, and subsequently be snowed under with schoolwork.

The reality was that they were just snowed under.

Many happy hours were spent in their igloos with a stash of sweets, though the dry nature of the snow left them unable to make decent snowballs, and therefore unable to defend their lairs from unwelcome visitors . . . namely me, the bearer of bad tidings, or at least the odd timely reminder that if they didn't do their schoolwork then there were going to be serious repercussions.

Detention after school was hardly an option, but a double lesson in home economics (namely peeling spuds and baking bread) seemed reasonable.

The sheep have coped well during this cold snap. Clive and I have been visiting them daily with bales of hay and sugar-beet pellets, and other than a few cases of blind illness (a type of conjunctivitis) everything was going well until a week ago (at the time of writing), when the temperature dropped to −12°C and the wind picked up. We awoke to drifts that covered walls, and the snow that had previously made the farm look as pretty as a picture now made getting out to the sheep at the moor nearly impossible.

We left Reuben, Sid and Miles to milk the house cow and muck out the cows, Edith and Violet feeding the calves and putting the milk through the sile. Raven lit the fire, and for the umpteenth time dressed the little ones in ski trousers and padded jackets and watched them head out into the winter wonderland. Clive and I got on the tractor and headed up to our most distant moorland heaf with a big bale of haylage and bags of feed. As we climbed, the drifts became ever deeper; the wind was savage.

We didn't get there. Part-way up the tractor slewed sideways, wheels spinning, snow flying in all directions. Clive swore, we whistled and sounded the horn and the sheep came running. A rough head count revealed that we were missing twenty, but there was no point in setting out to try and find them as conditions were so bad it was downright dangerous. We fed the flock and retreated, hoping for better things another day.

And so began a week of trudging through drifts that, in some places, were waist deep. With every step you sank through the crust; every night our footprints were erased by the wind-whipped snow, leaving no sign of the previous day's journey. During times such as these the sheepdogs would usually have been a great asset with their keen noses and boundless energy, but they could not travel, sinking beneath the snow's delicate surface and tiring fast.

We had all but given up on finding the missing twenty, and resigned ourselves to the fact that if they were still alive then we would have to wait until the weather receded to bring them home. The chances of them being buried were minimal, as although the snow was deep it was also light, and unlikely to lead to them being overblown.

Then seventeen-year-old Reuben phoned a friend. Reuben is mechanically-minded, inventive and intuitively able to see how things work; his friends are usually of a similar ilk. It turned out his friend, Martin, had a skidoo in his garage – and, what's more, he was happy to lend it to us to help us find our errant sheep. Sure enough, within hours, Martin was sitting in the farmyard on a bright yellow skidoo, giving Reuben instructions on its operation – which were basically the faster you go, the smoother the ride; top speed of 70mph, and lean in when cornering. So far we have located six of our wandering sheep; blown off their heaf, they were sheltering in a stone fold nearly a mile from the rest of the flock. The rest are unaccounted for as yet, but hope springs eternal.

A Tale from *The Dalesman*

Since I was a young lad I knew I always wanted to be a journalist – simple, really.

I'm nosy, enjoy meeting people and like writing – whether I'm any good at it is for others to decide.

And it's fair to say that for those near twenty-five years of 'being nosy' on local newspapers, armed with my metaphorical notepad and pen, I came to know much about how important the biggest-selling Yorkshire magazine, *The Dalesman*, is to the county.

An institution for more than eighty years, it's loved by legions of loyal readers all over the world, not just Yorkshire. So it wasn't lost on me how lucky I was to take up the editor's hotseat in October 2019, becoming only the seventh person to do so in the little magazine's big history.

It was on only my second day in post that I met a certain Amanda Owen when heading to Hudswell, near Richmond, to present *The Dalesman*'s Village of the Year prize, and she was clearly the star turn. Everyone in the packed pub wanted to talk to her. The TV cameras wanted her, and so did the other dignitaries.

Now it is at this point that I have to come clean and admit to not being much of an expert on Yorkshire's shepherdesses at the time. Okay, I knew Channel 5 keep hitting the back of the net with their programmes packed full of Yorkshirey goodness, so I was aware of *Our Yorkshire Farm*, as well as *The Yorkshire Vet* and now the reworking of *All Creatures Great and Small*. But, as my first days at *The Dalesman* turned into months, and now my first year, I have become acutely aware of how much love there is for Amanda, Clive and their youngsters.

They're charming, salt-of-the-earth, proper, honest people, so it's no wonder the regular TV insights into life up at Ravenseat are so popular with millions of viewers – it definitely explains why we sell such eye-watering numbers of Amanda's *Dalesman* calendars too!

I can't lay claim to having as many readers as Amanda has viewers, but I can confirm that both are a tremendously loyal bunch. I knew about our enviable reader loyalty, but I have been completely blown away at just how much they love their magazine. And following a year to forget, it's become even more apparent as time has worn on that *The Dalesman* has been a welcome distraction for many people.

Phone calls, emails and letters are easily into their hundreds every week (probably not as sizeable as Amanda's correspondence, admittedly), and I have the devil's own job to keep up with them all but, by hook or by crook, I just about manage it.

Many of the messages are quick to point out how important the magazine is in their lives. A number of these have reduced me to tears over the past months, I'm not ashamed to say.

I found out about 'Keith' following an email from his daughter wishing to cancel his subscription following his death.

She said in her email: 'Dad moved from his beloved Yorkshire in his twenties but always thought of North Yorkshire as his home. *The Dalesman* kept him in touch and he still felt a part of it. I sadly found Dad, who was clearly planning a lovely evening. He had poured himself a pint (in a straight glass, of course), got his supper ready and three editions of your magazine ready to read. *The Dalesman* was more than a magazine for Dad. Thank you.'

You can imagine my reaction upon reading that. But it's just an example of the deep feeling for the magazine.

I've also found out about three couples who were brought together as a direct result of the magazine, resulting in more than 125 years' happy marriage combined.

I heard from an elderly reader in London who has been isolated on her own during these Covid times, who wrote to me to simply thank us for continuing to produce the magazine – she rations herself to no more than three or four pages a day to make it last for the whole month.

And recently I had a lady write to say her husband had died and, with no family, she has been on her own in West Yorkshire, with various health problems.

But she, like so many others, took the time to write, and despite all her woes she simply wanted to say 'thank you' for the magazine she gets every month.

With no phone number provided, by the power of t'internet (Twitter, this time), and with the help of a kind police officer, Caroline, I managed to track her down to have some flowers delivered.

And now Ann – she won't mind the mention – has a visit every week from her new friend Caroline, and has become quite a celebrity in her neighbourhood with people keeping tabs on her.

So next time you hear someone bleating all the media is bad: not for our readers, it ain't. It's good (I hope), honest, wholesome stuff with no airs and graces, and simply celebrates the people, places and cultures of the white rose county every month.

Much the same can be said of Amanda and her family. So you can imagine my delight to realize the Yorkshire Shepherdess shares the same love for *The Dalesman* as our readers.

She 'gets' our readers – it's no surprise that she personally gave the winner of our 'design your own *Dalesman* front cover' competition a surprise phone call when the entry depicting Ravenseat was chosen by the judges as the winner.

And only recently, having heard some of the backstory of the aforementioned Ann from a chatty *Dalesman* editor, she called Ann for a natter.

Typical of our Amanda, that is.

Which makes it easy to forgive her being perilously close to deadline every single month – though, in all honesty, I have no idea how she manages to find time to do all her interviews and jobs around the farm *and* bring up her family.

So there you have it. *The Dalesman* and Amanda Owen – a match made in heaven, I reckon. I'd love to take the credit, but that's down to my predecessor, Adrian Braddy. I guarantee he'll miss being the first person to read her monthly scribblings – that pleasure now all mine, and which rarely fails to bring a smile to my face. Long may it continue.

I hope you enjoyed the enclosed 'tales from the farm', courtesy of Amanda and featuring her day-to-day trials and tribulations with Clive, Raven, Reuben, Miles, Edith, Violet, Sidney, Annas, Clemmy and Nancy.

So without going all 'Dalesman salesman', if you want to read about life on the Owen farm every month you know where to come – or if you know of someone who is exiled from their beloved Yorkshire, treat them to a subscription.

If you all do, I might even give Amanda a raise!

Yours in Yorkshire,
Jon Stokoe
Proud editor #7 of *The Dalesman* magazine

@jonstokoe
www.dalesman.co.uk

Keep up to date with Amanda in her monthly column in Yorkshire's favourite magazine

For our latest subscription offers

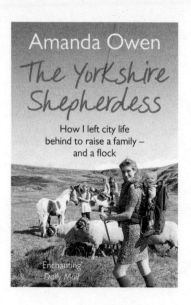

In her first book, *The Yorkshire Shepherdess*,
Amanda describes how the rebellious girl from Huddersfield,
who always wanted to be a shepherdess, achieved her dreams.
She shares funny stories of working as a contract shepherdess
and sometime alpaca shearer, meeting hill farmer Clive and
building a life with him at Ravenseat in Swaledale. She takes
us from fitting in with the locals to fitting in motherhood,
from the demands of the livestock to the demands of raising
a large family in such a remote part of the countryside.

'Riveting' *Sun*

A Year in the Life of the
**Yorkshire
Shepherdess**

1 husband, 8 children, 1,000 sheep...

Amanda Owen

'She, like her life, is extraordinary' Ben Fogle

In her second book, Amanda describes the age-old cycles of the farming year and the constant challenges she and her family face, from being cut off in winter to tending their flock on some of Yorkshire's highest, bleakest moors. Nine-year-old Miles gets his first flock, Reuben takes up the flugelhorn and she gives birth to a new baby girl. She is touched by the epic two-day journey of a mother sheep determined to find her lamb and gives a new home to an ageing and neglected horse. Meanwhile husband Clive is almost arrested on a midnight stakeout to catch a sheep-worrying dog and becomes the object of affection for a randy young bull.

'A really lovely, lyrical story of the ups and downs of their life' *Daily Mail*

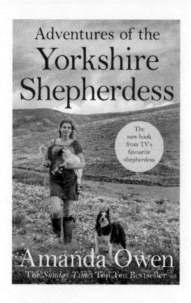

Adventures of the
Yorkshire
Shepherdess

The new book from TV's favourite shepherdess

Amanda Owen

The *Sunday Times* Top Ten Bestseller

In her third book Amanda takes us from her family's desperate race to save a missing calf to finding her bra has been repurposed as a house martin's nest, and from wild swimming to the brutal winter of 2018 that almost brought her to her knees. As busy as she is with her family and flock though, an exciting new project soon catches her eye . . . Ravenseat is a tenant farm and may not stay in the family, so when Amanda discovers a nearby farmhouse up for sale, she knows it is her chance to create roots for her children. The old house needs a lot of renovation and money is tight, so Amanda sets about the work herself, with some help from a travelling monk, a visiting plumber and Clive. It's fair to say things do not go according to plan!

'With its fizzing energy and celebration of nature and community, this is perfect comfort reading for uncertain times' *Daily Mail*